College Online

DATE DUE			
OE 19 '97			
MR 31 98			
OV 28 '98			
AG 5 99			
OC 7 00			
OE 10 00			

DEMCO 38-296

College Online
How to Take College Courses without Leaving Home

James P. Duffy

John Wiley & Sons, Inc.
New York • Chichester • Weinheim • Brisbane • Singapore • Toronto

This text is printed on acid-free paper.

Copyright © 1997 by James P. Duffy
Published by John Wiley & Sons, Inc.

This publication is designed to provide accurate and authoritative information in regard to the subject matter covered. It is sold with the understanding that the publisher is not engaged in rendering legal, accounting, or other professional services. If legal advice or other expert assistance is required, the services of a competent professional person should be sought.

Library of Congress Cataloging-in-Publication Data:

Duffy, James P.
     College online : how to take college courses without leaving home / James P. Duffy.
        p.   cm.
     Includes index.
     ISBN 0-471-12351-X (pbk. : alk. paper)
     1. Distance education—United States—Computer-assisted instruction.   2. University extension—United States—Computer-assisted instruction.   3. Education, Higher—United States—Computer-assisted instruction.   4. Education, Higher—United States—Computer-assisted instruction—Directories.   I. Title.
LC5803.C65D84   1997
378.175—dc20   96-34881

Printed in the United States of America

10   9   8   7   6   5   4   3   2   1

to Alexandra and Olivia

Contents

Acknowledgments   ix
Introduction   xi
Update   xiii

PART 1

Linking Your Computer to Your Future

Chapter 1   How Distance Learning Works   3
Education for the Twenty-First Century   3
Traditional and Nontraditional Education   6
Using the Correct Terms   11
The Value of Accreditation   13
Earning a Recognized Degree   21
The Many Ways You Can Earn Credits   23
How Online Courses Work   24
Deciding Whether Distance Learning Is Right for You   24

Chapter 2   How to Succeed at Independent Study   27
Reading: The Key to Learning   27
Proper Preparation for Exams   30
Scheduling Your Study Time   31
Learning Contracts and Degree Plans   34

Chapter 3   Selecting the Right Courses and Degree Program   39

Setting Goals and Getting Motivated   39
Committing Your Time   41
Assessing Your Ability   42
Selecting a Course or Program   43
Places to Save Your Credits   43

PART 2

The Electronic College Directories

Chapter 4   Directory of the Web Site Home Pages of North American Colleges and Universities   47

The Internet, The Web, and You   47

Chapter 5   Directory of Undergraduate and Graduate College Courses Available Online   73

The Easy-to-Use Online College Course Locator   74
How to Read the Descriptions   92
Full Descriptions of Online College Courses   93

Chapter 6   Directory of Undergraduate and Graduate Degree Programs Available Online   193

The Easy-to-Use Online Degree Program Locator   194
How to Read the Descriptions   198
Full Descriptions of Online Degree Programs   199

Appendix A

Scholarships Online   217

Appendix B

A Virtual University in the Making   219

Index   221

Acknowledgments

A book such as this one is dependent on the contributions of so many people that it would be impossible to list them all without accidentally leaving someone out, a slight I would prefer to avoid. So, instead of a long list, I want to express my appreciation to the many people at the colleges and universities throughout North America who provided the information contained in these pages. In addition to those people who so generously provided information on their courses and answered my many questions, I want to extend a special thanks to Jeff Herman, for his continued excellent representation, to Judith McCarthy and Chris Jackson, for their incredible patience, to Paula Ruffino, who did such a fine job with the screen captures used in this volume, to my wife, Kathleen, for her understanding that makes every effort possible, and to Alexandra and Olivia, for their smiles and love.

Introduction

Imagine yourself sitting down at your home or office computer with a cup of coffee and taking a college course. The course may be one that will help you earn your undergraduate degree or even your master's or doctorate. Or it might simply be on a subject that interests you. That's right—you can now enroll in and take college courses from the comfort of your own home, or even your office if you like. In fact, you can now take college courses from anywhere in the world, using your own or someone else's computer. The Internet and the World Wide Web have made it incredibly easy for anyone with a modem to reach hundreds of fully accredited colleges and universities throughout the United States.

This book shows you how you can use your computer to take college courses and even earn a degree from an accredited college or university. You need never attend a class or even set foot on the campus of the college that awards you your degree. You need never sit face to face with your professors to learn from them, even though you may have interesting and insightful conversations with them. It is all done through your computer.

You do not have to be a computer expert to take the courses described in this book: you need only have the ability to use the basic functions of your computer required to travel across the now-famous information highway and reach out to the computer at your college. Even if you have no online experience, it is really basic stuff and can be mastered in a day.

This book is divided into two parts. Part One introduces you to the world of distance learning. In this part you will find valuable information concerning taking nontraditional college courses, such as online courses. You will also discover tips on studying that will help you learn more in less time and how to find and select the courses that will aid you most in reaching your goals. You will also find useful details concerning how to prepare for examinations, for even online courses require students to take examinations; how to schedule your study most productively; and the many other nontraditional ways in which you can take college courses and earn college credits.

Part Two contains the directories that will make it possible for you to reach the college of your choice and take the online course you want or enroll in the online program through which you can earn a degree. The first chapter in this part is a directory of college and university home pages; the second chapter in this part contains descriptions of nearly 500 college courses you can take online. The last chapter includes in-depth information about almost 100 undergraduate and graduate degree programs you can take online.

Before you press that button on your computer and begin the first step toward enrolling in an online course, take the time to read Part One. The information it contains will help you reach your educational goals.

Update

As the number of colleges and universities that begin offering online communications grows each month, keeping track of what courses and degree programs are available online is a task of monumental proportions. In an effort to maintain the most current information for future editions of this book, anyone with information concerning changes in the present offerings or new offerings is asked to forward that information to the author at the following address:

James P. Duffy
℅ John Wiley & Sons, Inc.
Professional and Trade Division
605 Third Avenue
New York, NY 10158-0012

PART 1

Linking Your Computer to Your Future

1 How Distance Learning Works

EDUCATION FOR THE TWENTY-FIRST CENTURY

A college degree has become an invaluable credential for a rapidly increasing number of professions. In fact, in most fields the absence of a degree can stunt an otherwise promising career. Unfortunately for many thousands of working adults, the commitments involved in maintaining a career, along with the pressures and demands of family life, form virtually insurmountable obstacles to returning to school to earn the degree they need.

Recognizing this dilemma, many fully accredited colleges and universities now offer a wide variety of nontraditional programs leading to bachelor's or master's degrees that do not place the usual time and residence demands on adult learners. These are external and nontraditional programs that culminate in the awarding of bachelor's and advanced degrees that allow you to do most or all of your work at home, at times that are convenient to you. Many degree programs offered by accredited universities now use correspondence courses, televised courses, online courses, proficiency examinations, independent study projects, and numerous other methods of learning outside the traditional classroom environment.

The opportunity for adults to further their formal education has never been better than it is now, so take advantage of the programs described in this book, find the right degree program for you and your career, and begin earning that college degree today while you continue in your present job.

Following publication of the first edition of my book on external college degree programs in 1983, I was deluged by hundreds of people asking the identical question: "Is it really possible to earn a college degree without going to college?" The answer was—and it is even more emphatically the answer today—"Absolutely!" A college or university degree is no longer considered a luxury within reach of only the well-to-do. A college degree is now an important credential for anyone, in almost all walks of life. In the business world, especially, it is taken as testimony of serious achievement.

In recent years, colleges and universities throughout the country have expanded their services in an effort to attract new students. As they did this, educators became aware of an entirely new type of prospective student. This is the person who, for any of a variety of reasons, is unable to attend formal scheduled classes—often an adult who is raising a family. Commitments to job, home, and family prevent these individuals from achieving the level of formal education they want and need.

In response to the needs of these people, educational institutions began to modify the traditional class schedule. Evening and weekend classes soon became a regular part of the instructional offerings at most colleges and universities. Adults flocked to them in numbers that almost overwhelmed many schools. It quickly became obvious that these colleges had begun to tap a huge source of students.

Many of these new students, however, were disenchanted with what they found in the classroom. Experienced adults found themselves forced to sit through classes on subjects that they knew as well as, or even better than, their instructors. Business executives with no formal education in finance, accounting, labor relations, or other subjects related to their careers discovered that the knowledge they had gained while earning a living was equivalent to or sometimes more extensive than that offered in college courses they were taking. For many, this adversely affected their motivation. Some dropped out of the classes from boredom, while others trudged through, doing time so they could earn credits toward their degrees.

Self-motivation was a primary mover among those students enrolled in these continuing education classes. Teaching them what they already knew was not the answer to their needs. Scheduling was also a problem for many adult students who were forced to miss classes because of work requirements such as late hours or travel. Another solution was needed.

During the late 1950s and early 1960s, a major step was taken to deal with adult learners who had acquired knowledge comparable to that realized through a college course. This was the introduction of examinations that tested and evaluated a person's knowledge and equated it to college learning. The results individuals achieved on these examinations could earn them college-level credits equal to those they would have earned if they had attended classes and passed end-of-term examinations.

Actually, this was an innovation only in the United States. Many old and famous European institutions of higher learning had followed this practice for years. Earning credits, or even a degree, depended not on the amount of time you spent in a classroom but on the knowledge you demonstrated in an examination. Imaginative educators in the U.S. began to experiment with these examinations and other nontraditional ways to earn college-level credits. Soon it became possible for individuals to earn a substantial portion of the credits required for a degree through these methods.

The next step, and a major breakthrough for persons who desired a college degree but who found regular class attendance difficult, came in September 1970. During his inauguration that month as president of the University of the State of New York and as state commissioner of education, Ewald B. Nyquist suggested the establishment of the Regents External Degree Program under the sponsorship of the Board of Regents of the university. With the endorsement of that body, the first truly external degree program in the United States became available. In 1972, the Regents External Degree Program conferred degrees on seventy-seven graduates. That program, now known as Regents College, has since awarded over 55,000 degrees to graduates from every state in the union and dozens of countries around the world. And Regents College is only one among the distinguished group of colleges and universities offering external degree programs.

There are numerous ways in which you can earn college credits without attending classes. Among the nontraditional methods are proficiency examinations, which test your knowledge of a specific subject and compare it to the knowledge one would acquire attending a traditional college class on the same subject; experiential learning, which is learning acquired through the activities of your life, such as work, hobbies, reading, travel, and so on; correspondence courses, which permit you to bring a college class into your home so you can study at times and places convenient to you; and noncollegiate education, which might be company training programs, courses taken during military service, or courses offered by labor unions, a local museum or library, or dozens of other sources of knowledge you might not normally think could lead to earning college credits toward your degree.

The newest and perhaps most exciting innovation in the delivery of college courses are the online programs discussed in this book. These programs allow you to go online and receive course materials, messages, and evaluations from your professors at your personal computer. Many of these programs have a conferencing system that allows you to "talk" with fellow students almost as if you were all in the same room, and because most information is stored in electronic mailboxes, you can all talk to each other asynchronously, that is, at different times of the day, to suit the convenience of the sender and the receiver.

The use of personal computers to take college classes and even earn degrees is rapidly spreading through academia. So, if you own a computer and have access to the Internet, you may find that at least some, if not all, the courses you need to earn your degree can be taken through your computer.

If you discover that you cannot complete all your degree requirements through online courses, or the degree programs available online are not to your liking, then you should consider the other nontraditional methods discussed in two of my other books, *How to Earn a College Degree without Going to College* and *How to Earn an Advanced Degree without Going to Graduate School.* The latest editions of both these books were published in 1994 by John Wiley and Sons, Inc. The first includes a directory of over 600 undergraduate external degree programs. The second reviews nearly 150 external and nontraditional programs leading to master's and doctoral degrees from accredited colleges, universities, and graduate schools. The programs in both books require little or no actual classroom attendance.

TRADITIONAL AND NONTRADITIONAL EDUCATION

Not many years ago, earning an academic degree without spending a great deal of time in college or university classrooms was virtually impossible. Within the past two decades, however, dramatic changes in the delivery of educational services have occurred. A transformation has come about not only in the basic concept of how a quality education can be provided, but also in who provides it and where and how the process takes place.

Traditional colleges and universities have become increasingly aggressive in their pursuit of students. A glance through almost any newspaper will yield several advertisements from local colleges. Most are aimed at adults, enticing them to enroll for the first time or to return to college. They offer help in achieving career-advancement goals, making career changes, or generally improving one's life through study. The less-than-promising supply of new high school graduates has made working adults the new clientele, eagerly sought after by institutions of higher education.

The number of adults returning to the educational process has been so great and has had such impact on the system that it has spawned an entire generation of educators devoted to alternative and continuing education to serve them. Because these students bring with them the problems and responsibilities of adulthood, most are insistent that their educational programs meet their needs, in terms of both *what* is taught and *when* and *where* it is taught. The proliferation of weekend and evening courses and the use of off-campus facilities give clear evidence that colleges and universities are expanding their traditional schedules to meet the demands of adult educational consumers. Colleges and universities now regularly conduct their classes in union halls, high schools, storefront classrooms, and other nontraditional places where learners can gather comfortably.

More than class schedules have been altered, however, by the rising number of adult students. Adults are eager to play a major role in developing their own educational programs and are prepared to switch schools when they feel their needs are not being met. They are serious about their education and expect the school to which they pay their money to be serious about it, too.

The response to this consumer awareness in higher education has been a sharing of responsibility between the school and the student in developing the student's educational plan. For example, those students enrolled in the College of New Rochelle's School of New Resources, which specializes in higher education for adults, are required to attend two degree-planning seminars. One is scheduled when the student has earned 30 credits and the other after 60 credits. With the aid of an academic advisor, each student develops a degree plan based on personal needs. These plans are intended to help students chart their own academic careers. Many of the institutions offering external degree programs, including several with online programs, require students to work with faculty advisors to design their own degree plans.

Dean Margaret Olson of Empire State College points to two illustrations of the impact that adults have had on higher education. First, college applications rarely include space anymore for the name of one's high school guidance counselor. Second, most colleges no longer require that all students enroll in at least one physical education course.

With adult learners representing a multibillion-dollar business, it was only a matter of time until traditional colleges and universities would be confronted by competition from outside the educational community. Although corporations and industries have traditionally conducted internal training programs for their own employees, that sort of training began growing considerably during the late 1970s and early 1980s. In 1985, the Carnegie Foundation for the Advancement of Teaching estimated that expenditures for these programs exceeded $60 billion a year. Although the recession of the late 1980s and early 1990s had a negative impact on that expenditure, it remains a substantial amount. A new twist on this type of training is the establishment of degree-granting institutions that are affiliated with established business corporations. A Carnegie Foundation study released in 1985 found eighteen corporate or industry associations awarding academic degrees that were—or soon would be— regionally accredited.

The bottom line of all this activity is that higher education has become a more flexible process. This flexibility does not reflect a decline in the quality of the education or in the value of academic credentials earned through nontraditional methods. If anything, it has helped to bring the process closer to the realities of life encountered by students and graduates.

Among the most important changes resulting from this flexibility is the recognition that learning takes place in many environments, not just in the classroom. This recognition, coupled with the increased demands of individuals seeking academic credit for knowledge they have already acquired, or can acquire, outside the classroom, gave birth to a new field of alternative higher education. As a result, a person can now earn a bachelor's, a master's, or even a doctoral degree from an accredited institution located on hundreds of acres of manicured lawns with thousands of students in attendance, without ever stepping foot onto the campus to attend a class. These colleges include esteemed state-supported universities and highly regarded private institutions. A rapidly increasing number of them are making use of online courses and online programs. Several hundred more colleges, while not offering external degree programs, do provide adult learners with formal but nontraditional methods of earning credits toward a degree.

Each year, thousands of adults earn bachelor's degrees through external and other nontraditional programs. A federally funded survey found that more than half the graduates from external undergraduate degree programs go on to advanced degree study. Joining these external degree program graduates are other adults, already engaged in their professional careers, returning to the education process to broaden their knowledge and improve their credentials.

It was only logical that these adult learners would bring other changes into the process of earning a college degree. Working men and women are usually unable to step out of the employment market for several years to attend a school; few can afford the out-of-pocket costs and the loss of immediate income involved in such a commitment. Many colleges and universities responded by scheduling degree programs based on evening and weekend classes and by creating external undergraduate and graduate degree programs.

As more businesses and other organizations require job candidates to hold degrees for higher paying positions, many individuals who never attended college or never completed the requirements for a degree recognize the need to upgrade their educational credentials. For many people, a college degree has become necessary if they are to achieve their career goals. However, the need to continue active employment combined with job and family responsibilities precludes most adults from attending school full-time. The external degree programs are helping to alleviate this frequent and frustrating problem.

The *Oxford American Dictionary* defines a degree as "an academic rank awarded to a person who has successfully completed a course of study." *Good's Dictionary of Education* says that an academic degree "is conferred by an institution of higher education, regardless of the field of study."

The first recorded reference to an academic degree dates to mid-twelfth-century Italy, when the University of Bologna conferred a doctorate. The use of degrees soon spread among the principal European universities, where bachelorships, masterships, and doctorates were the most commonly awarded. The University of Bologna's first doctorates were in civil law. Later, doctorates in canon law and divinity were added, followed in the thirteenth century by medicine, grammar, logic, and philosophy. Two centuries later, the universities at Oxford and Cambridge in England conferred doctorates in music. Degrees began to proliferate until there were 633 in use by universities of the British Commonwealth in the mid-twentieth century.

Harvard College was the first American institution to confer a degree. Because most of its founders and governing board members were graduates of Cambridge, it was natural that they should follow the British custom. The pattern they set eventually spread to other American colleges and universities. Now this process has arrived at an educational system designed to meet the needs of adult students in the twenty-first century. The most recent manifestation of this continuing evolvement is the online external degree program.

In truth, there are no external degrees; there are only external degree programs, including the online programs in this book. The diploma you earn through the colleges and universities sponsoring the programs reviewed in this book, as well as my earlier books, is identical in every way to the diploma awarded to graduates of the traditional classroom-based programs of those institutions. No institution to my knowledge inserts the words "external degree" on any degree they confer. The only difference between a college degree earned through traditional, or "regular," class attendance and one earned through an online or other external degree program is found in the methods used to earn the required number of college-level credits.

A degree awarded by an external degree program is one that can be earned with little or no time in formal classes. All, or most, learning takes place through nontraditional methods, such as online. All the degrees explained in this book are awarded by institutions of higher learning that have been granted a form of recognition known as accreditation. This recognition can be one of the most important aspects of your college degree.

Some people who enroll in external degree programs never complete the requirements for the degree they seek. This is because they entered the program under the impression that it was an easy way to earn a college degree. For most people, this is not the case. To be a successful online student you must be well motivated and have enough self-discipline to alter your current life-style to meet the demands of studying and taking exams. It may be less time-consuming than traditional degree routes, but it is not necessarily easier. It may be especially difficult for those who require the competition of a classroom environment or the close attention of an instructor to do well.

USING THE CORRECT TERMS

You may encounter a number of unfamiliar terms and phrases when taking online college courses or pursuing a college degree through online courses or other nontraditional methods. The most common of these are *external degree program, nontraditional* or *innovative program* (both presently used interchangeably to describe a wide range of programs), and *alternative education.*

What one institution calls its "independent study program," another characterizes as "nontraditional." Two programs that have little relationship to each other in their mode of operation can both be portrayed as "nonresidential." In most institutions that offer them, independent study programs are based on credit-bearing correspondence courses. Unfortunately, the term is also used to describe programs that incorporate no correspondence courses. Some colleges shun the term "correspondence courses," preferring instead to call their courses that operate in the identical way as "distance learning courses," or "faculty directed courses," or a half dozen other terms.

External degree program is defined in the first chapter, but it will be helpful to paraphrase that definition here. This is a program in which the individual student plays a role in developing the curriculum, and the program is not based on typical class participation but recognizes learning acquired in other environments. What constitutes "class participation," however, remains vague in many cases. Some so-called external degree programs require the participant to attend so many classes or seminars that the institution has stretched the term beyond recognition. On the other hand, there are programs called "independent" or "innovative" that are actually full-fledged external degree programs, many requiring no time on campus at all.

Alternative education is also a term that has been too broadly applied, although less so because it is difficult to label a course based on class attendance as alternative, although some have tried. Alternative education is a form of learning that substitutes for traditional classroom education. A correspondence course, tutorial, off-campus seminar, independently conducted research project, guided self-study, and internship can all justifiably be classified as methods of alternative education, as can the use of proficiency examinations. These forms of learning are discussed in depth in later chapters.

Another form of learning that can only be classified as alternative education is experiential. It takes place outside any formal program. Sometimes called life experience, it consists of learning you have acquired from your job, hobby, reading, noncredit courses, volunteer work, or virtually any other activity that has increased your knowledge. Those institutions willing to recognize the value of that learning will grant college-level credits for it following an assessment of your knowledge, not your experience. The assessment is used to determine what you have learned from your experiences and whether that learning is equivalent to what you would have been expected to learn from a more formal structured form of education, such as a college course. This is explained in detail later.

Alternative education encompasses all learning methods other than the traditional but provides a comparable level of knowledge. An alternative education program, if named properly, is one in which all, or a substantial amount, of the learning takes place other than through traditional class instruction.

As you can see, a measure of imprecision characterizes the terminology used by colleges, universities, and graduate schools to describe programs that are not based on traditional residential study. In an effort to bring some order to this entire subject, and to aid the reader in locating the most suitable program, this book draws an arbitrary line between college degree programs that are justifiably entitled to the name external graduate degree programs and those that are nontraditional but not strictly external.

The difference between these two classifications is the amount of time a participant is required to spend in classes, or in residence. Some external degree programs have no residency requirements at all; others stipulate a minimal amount of time that participants must spend at seminars or planning sessions. If the time one is required to spend at the school either is of short duration or can be arranged in such a manner that it would be compatible with the schedules of most working people, that program is included in this book. Also included are programs requiring on-campus time long enough to interfere with the typical work schedule but still short enough to make the program attractive to those readers whose schedules are either substantially different or more flexible than the average.

Until there is more uniformity in the definitions of these terms, all of them will continue to be subject to misuse. Independent study is really a form of learning that the student accomplishes basically alone, without a face-to-face instructor or a formal classroom environment. Online courses and correspondence courses are two forms of independent study. Nonresidential programs are those that do not require students to be in residence at the sponsoring institution. A nontraditional program is one that offers a mode of learning that is different from the traditional classroom method. Unfortunately, the blurred lines among these programs continue to create confusion, which in turn is compounded by the occasional complete misuse of a term, such as when a college describes a program that requires fifty percent of a student's time be spent attending on-campus classes as "nonresidential."

THE VALUE OF ACCREDITATION

With the exception of the military academies and certain institutions in the District of Columbia, authorization for the operation of a degree-granting college or university is the responsibility of the individual states. The requirements of each state for the approval of college charters vary widely. Some states, most notably New York, are extremely strict when it comes to authorizing the awarding of an academic degree. Unfortunately, though, many states have little or no real control over the independent degree-granting institutions that operate within their borders.

Potential participants in a nontraditional educational program must be concerned about the validity and recognition of the academic credentials earned. The examples of two states, New York and California, show wide differences in the way in which states grant authority to institutions of higher education.

New York exercises tight control over all educational institutions through the University of the State of New York. This university is an umbrella organization that includes all public and independent colleges and universities, elementary and secondary schools, libraries, museums, historical societies, other educational agencies within the state, and any other organization that describes itself as "educational." Established in 1784, the University of the State of New York is presided over by the Board of Regents, which "determines the State's educational policies, establishes standards for maintaining quality in the schools, incorporates colleges and universities, approves and supervises academic programs leading to college degrees, licenses and establishes standards for most professions, and confers diplomas and degrees." All institutions of higher education must meet the same standards established by the Board of Regents in order to operate in the state.

California approaches higher educational institutions differently. For years it used a multilevel system for permitting the granting of degrees. The superintendent of public instruction classified a college or university as "exempt" (usually religious), "accredited," "approved," or "authorized." This situation made the state the home for a wide variety of unaccredited schools, including several excellent nontraditional colleges, but it also became the headquarters for hundreds of diploma mills and other questionable operations. Under pressure caused by numerous news stories, the state took some steps to clean up its act, but they were tentative and have not yet had substantial results. California appears to have been replaced as the home of diploma mills by Hawaii, which has been lax in regulating schools of any type, including those operating out of secretarial services and spare bedrooms.

A review of the various state laws and regulations concerning the operation of private and independent degree-granting institutions and the widespread apparent lack of educational standards aimed at protecting students makes it clear that potential participants in nontraditional graduate and undergraduate programs must be sure that the school in which they enroll is legitimate and that the degree they earn will be recognized as a valuable result of a worthwhile education.

In the absence of reliable information from many states on the schools within their jurisdictions, and being conscious of your need for academic credentials of unquestionable quality, this book includes only those institutions that have been accredited by a recognized accrediting association. This does not imply that all unaccredited schools are inferior; remember that every school was at some time unaccredited. It simply means that some acknowledged authority has given its blessing to the accredited school or program in question.

An institution's accreditation may indeed be one of the most important factors you consider when selecting any college or university. Not only is it important to know that a school is accredited; you will also want to know who accredited it. It is not uncommon for diploma mill operators to create their own accrediting authority for the sole purpose of granting a worthless accreditation to their phony "college." Being able to claim that their school is "fully accredited" surely does not hurt sales.

When educators speak of accreditation, they are usually referring to recognition accorded by one of the accrediting associations that are in turn recognized by either the Council on Recognition of Postsecondary Accreditation (CORPA), a voluntary nongovernmental organization, or the U.S. Department of Education, through The Accrediting Agency Evaluation Branch of the Office of Postsecondary Education. This recognition of accrediting associations is used primarily to help establish eligibility for federal student aid programs. All accrediting associations are recognized by CORPA or the U.S. Department of Education, or both.

CORPA was formed in 1975 by the merger of six accrediting organizations, including the Federation of Regional Accrediting Commissions of Higher Education and the National Commission on Accrediting. There are presently seventy accrediting bodies recognized by CORPA, and more than 4,000 institutions that are accredited or seeking accreditation by them. It is governed by a twenty-four-member board of directors. Members of the board represent the accrediting agencies, accredited institutions, educational associations, and the general public.

The majority of institution-wide accrediting, meaning the accreditation of the school as a whole institution, is done by six regional accrediting associations, although some specialized schools are accredited by national accrediting bodies. Individual programs or departments within a college may be accredited by one of the specialized accrediting associations that are concerned with education leading to specific professions. In many professions, it is equally important, and sometimes of greater importance, that a specific program or department be accredited by the profession's accrediting body than the institution be regionally accredited.

One of those regional bodies, the Middle States Association of Colleges and Schools, through its Commission on Higher Education, defines accreditation as "an expression of confidence in an institution's mission and goals, performance and resources." It continues, "Accreditation rests on the integrity with which institutions conduct their educational endeavors and the policies they establish for ensuring their quality."

The process through which an institution receives accreditation is a time-consuming and arduous one. It starts when the school makes written application to the appropriate regional or national association. Accreditation is strictly voluntary; no institution is required to participate, although it would seem rather foolish for any legitimate well-run school not to seek that recognition of its quality.

Preliminary investigations of the school are conducted, followed by visits from representatives of the regional associations. These representatives prepare written reports of their evaluations of specific areas, such as previous preparation of students, effectiveness of admissions procedures, training and performance of the faculty and administrative officers, the quality of the relationship between those two staffs, the fitness and range of the curriculum in relation to the institution's stated goals, size and suitability of the library, condition of the physical facilities, and financial resources of the school.

During this process, the school moves through several stages until it reaches recognition as a "candidate for accreditation" and, finally, becomes an "accredited institution." Periodic visits are made to all accredited institutions to ensure that they continue to meet the association's standards.

Every college or university that is accredited by a recognized accrediting association will state so in its catalog or descriptive brochure. The following is an example of an accreditation statement: "California State University Dominguez Hills is accredited by the Western Association of Schools and Colleges."

In some professions, a degree from an accredited institution receives only partial recognition if the department or program through which the degree was earned is not accredited by the appropriate specialized accrediting association. So, if you want the maximum recognition for your degree, check the listing at the end of this chapter to see whether there is a professional specialized accrediting body in your chosen field. If so, ask the school in which you are considering enrolling about this additional accreditation. Most of the specialized accrediting associations will be happy to send you a list of the schools, programs, and departments that have been accredited by them.

Participating in a program sponsored by an institution that has not been accredited by a recognized accrediting association is a decision only you can make. Remember that the process of accreditation can take several years, so a fairly new school must operate without accreditation for that period. Remember, too, that accreditation, although of obvious value to a school, is purely voluntary.

If, for whatever reason, you decide that your best opportunity to earn the degree you seek is from an unaccredited college or university, here are some steps you should take to be sure that you are dealing with a legitimate institution granting a degree that will be of value to you. Before beginning these steps, however, you must know how knowledgeable people in your chosen field perceive this school and its degrees. Often it is as important where you earned your degree as is the fact you earned it.

First, contact the school and ask why it is not accredited. You may be told that accreditation has been applied for and is in the process of being secured. If so, find out which association is conducting the evaluation. If the accrediting body is listed in this chapter, call or write, explaining that you are considering enrolling in the school in question and ask about the status of its application for accreditation. If the accrediting body is not listed in this chapter, ask the college for its address and telephone number. Write and ask about their authority to grant accreditation and their relationship, if any, to either CORPA or the U.S. Department of Education. If you receive no reply, look for another college.

But what about colleges and universities that acknowledge they are not accredited and have no desire to be? They may have a legitimate reason for not seeking accreditation or may have been refused accreditation for some reason that is acceptable to you. Do not hesitate to express your concern about the school's lack of accreditation, and do not be satisfied with an off-hand reply, such as "accreditation doesn't mean anything." It does. Remember, it is not just your money, time, and effort that you are investing in this school. A degree from a disreputable school can be damaging to your career.

When you have received satisfactory responses to your questions on accreditation, go a step farther. Find out how many students are enrolled at the college, ask about the size and backgrounds of the faculty, learn how many graduates the school has had, and try to obtain the names and addresses of recent degree recipients in your field. Some institutions may have a policy against releasing this information, but if they recognize the concerns prospective students have about accreditation, they should change those policies so their graduates can attest to the quality of the education they received. If they do give you names, contact them.

If you are satisfied with the answers you receive, one final place to check for information is the agency responsible for regulating institutions of higher education in the state in which the school is located. As mentioned earlier, a number of states maintain little control over independent colleges and universities, but it is worth asking them about the legal standing of the school and whether they have had any complaints about the institution.

Having earned it from an accredited department or program within an accredited institution might be one of the most significant factors about your degree. Before considering an unaccredited school, take into consideration how others in your field or prospective employers will view your degree. Receiving an excellent education and a degree from an unaccredited institution may be of substantially less value if the professionals in your field have lower regard for your degree than one earned from an accredited school.

The following list is divided into two categories: those associations that accredit an entire institution throughout the nation are listed first, followed by the regional associations that also accredit entire institutions, but only within their assigned regions. A third category, which is not included in this list, is associations that accredit specific departments or programs within a college or university. This specialized accreditation is usually done by professional groups dedicated to maintaining the highest standards in the education of those entering their professions.

Each of the following associations will send you, on request, a list of all colleges, universities, and/or departments that have been accredited by them.

NATIONAL INSTITUTIONAL ACCREDITING

Bible Colleges

American Association of Bible Colleges (CORPA) (USDE)
P.O. Box 1523
Fayetteville, AR 72701
(501) 521-8164
Fax: (501) 521-9202

Business Colleges

Career College Association (CORPA) (USDE)
750 First Street, NE, Suite 900
Washington, DC 20002-4242
(202) 336-6700
Fax: (202) 842-2593

Home Study Institutions

Distance Education and Training Council (CORPA) (USDE)
1601 Eighteenth Street, NW
Washington, DC 20009
(202) 234-5100
Fax: (202) 332-1386

Rabbinical and Talmudic Schools

Association of Advanced Rabbinical & Talmudic Schools (CORPA) (USDE)
175 Fifth Avenue, Room 711
New York, NY 10010
(212) 477-0950
Fax: (212) 533-5335

Theology

Association of Theological Schools in the U.S. & Canada (CORPA) (USDE)
10 Summitt Park Drive
Pittsburgh, PA 15275-1103
(412) 788-6505
Fax: (412) 788-6510

Trade and Technical Schools

Career College Association (CORPA) (USDE)
750 First Street, NW, Suite 900
Washington, DC 20002-4242
(202) 336-6700
Fax: (202) 842-2585

REGIONAL INSTITUTIONAL ACCREDITING

Middle States Association of Colleges & Schools (CORPA) (USDE)
3624 Market Street
Philadelphia, PA 19104
(215) 662–5606
Fax: (215) 662–5950

Includes Delaware, District of Columbia, Maryland, New Jersey, New York, Pennsylvania, Puerto Rico, and Virgin Islands.

New England Association of Schools & Colleges (CORPA) (USDE)
15 High Street
Winchester, MA 01890
(617) 729–6762
Fax: (617) 729–0924

Includes Connecticut, Maine, Massachusetts, New Hampshire, Rhode Island, and Vermont.

North Central Association of Colleges & Schools (CORPA) (USDE)
159 North Dearborn Street
Chicago, IL 60601
(312) 263–0456
Fax: (312) 263–7462

Includes Arizona, Arkansas, Colorado, Illinois, Indiana, Iowa, Kansas, Michigan, Minnesota, Missouri, Nebraska, New Mexico, North Dakota, Ohio, Oklahoma, South Dakota, West Virginia, Wisconsin, and Wyoming.

Northwest Association of Schools & Colleges (CORPA) (USDE)
3700–B University Way, NE
Seattle, WA 98105
(206) 543–0195
Fax: (206) 685–4621

Includes Alaska, Idaho, Montana, Nevada, Oregon, Utah, and Washington.

Southern Association of Colleges & Schools (CORPA) (USDE)
1866 Southern Lane
Decatur, GA 30033–4097
(404) 679–4500
Fax: (404) 679–4558

Includes Alabama, Florida, Georgia, Kentucky, Louisiana, Mississippi, North Carolina, South Carolina, Tennessee, Texas, and Virginia.

Western Association of Schools & Colleges (CORPA) (USDE)
P.O. Box 70
3060 Valencia Avenue
Aptos, CA 95003
(408) 688-7575
Fax: (408) 688-1841

Includes California, Guam, and Hawaii.

SPECIALIZED ACCREDITING

For information concerning the groups that are recognized for having the responsibility of accrediting specific programs or departments, contact either or both of the following:

The Council on Recognition of Postsecondary Accreditation
One Dupont Circle, Suite 305
Washington, DC 20036
(202) 452-1433
Fax: (202) 331-9571

Request a copy of the Membership Directory.

U.S. Department of Education
Office of Postsecondary Education
Washington, DC 20202-5171
(202) 708-7417

Request a copy of Nationally Recognized Accrediting Agencies and Associations.

Both publications are free, and both list recognized accrediting associations.

EARNING A RECOGNIZED DEGREE

Most people who are considering using nontraditional methods of earning college credits or earning a degree ask about the true value of a degree earned nontraditionally. What they want to know is how others, especially employers, view a degree earned outside the traditional classroom. Perhaps the best way to answer this question, which should be a major concern to prospective external degree students, is to look at the experiences of those who have already earned their degrees and used them as credentials just as any other college graduate would.

There are two arenas college graduates typically enter after graduation, the world of work and graduate school. Explaining how employers view the degrees it offers through its external degree program, Elizabethtown College reports: "Our experience with over 200 graduates indicates that when employers are given an explanation of the program they regard the degrees in the same manner as traditional college degrees. In fact, many employers help underwrite the employee's costs in earning the adult external degree."

A broader view of external degree program graduates is provided by the Bureau of Social Science Research. This study is summed up as follows: "In the world of work, the external degree yielded tangible benefits for the majority of degree holders. Women as a group profited especially, as did those who were at the lower end of the occupational spectrum prior to degree completion."

The study also found considerable employer interest in the educational objectives and accomplishments of employees. Interest was so great that almost one-third of the external degree graduates surveyed indicated they received some financial assistance from their employers to help defray the costs of earning their degrees.

There is another factor that must be taken into consideration when an employer looks at an external degree program graduate for a prospective job or promotion, providing the candidate explains how the degree was earned. Earning a degree through alternative methods is not an easy task. The holder of this degree has demonstrated substantial self-motivation. The work to earn the degree, whether taking examinations or studying through correspondence courses, takes time from the normal activities of life. There is a significant amount of sacrifice by the external degree student. Justifiable pride in having accomplished what was required in terms of both time and effort is not uncommon in external degree program graduates.

Acceptance into graduate school is based on a large number of factors. It is difficult to assess how much effect having earned an undergraduate degree through an external degree program has on an applicant's admission to graduate school. The majority of colleges and universities sponsoring external degree programs report that high percentages of their graduates go on to advanced study at accredited graduate schools. Many a catalog proudly lists the graduate schools that have accepted external degree program graduates.

The Bureau of Social Science Research study mentioned previously found that over half of the external degree program graduates questioned had entered into advanced study programs at the graduate level. The study also found that the external degree ". . . did not constitute an obstacle to obtaining further education." With so many respected graduate schools and graduate programs at large universities now offering external graduate degree programs, it is hard to imagine any administrator or admissions committee failing to recognize the value of having earned an undergraduate degree through an external degree program.

Earning your degree through an external or nontraditional program is something you will be proud of, because successful completion of one of these programs requires an individual to be well motivated, a self-starter, self-disciplined, and able to set and achieve realistic goals and to work independently of direct supervision. These are all personal attributes every employer knows are extremely valuable. Dr. Homer Babbidge, former assistant secretary of Health, Education, and Welfare and former dean of the Harvard Graduate Center, considers a degree earned through an external program to be "an excellent index of the single most important quality for success—motivation."

THE MANY WAYS YOU CAN EARN CREDITS

In addition to the online courses described in this book, there are several other nontraditional methods you can use to earn the undergraduate or graduate degree you seek. Some of these methods have already been discussed, but including them here in one place will help you decide whether any are appropriate for your needs and goals. There are over 600 external degree programs from accredited colleges and universities leading to undergraduate degrees and about 150 leading to graduate degrees. They all include at least some of the options available through nontraditional education.

Ways of earning undergraduate- and graduate-level credits include taking correspondence courses, passing proficiency examinations, completing portfolios of experiential learning or learning from your own life experiences, and taking courses offered by companies and associations. These are only the major options available to you once you decide on using nontraditional methods for earning credits or even a degree. Many colleges and universities offer additional paths to reach your goal.

HOW ONLINE COURSES WORK

For the most part, the online courses and programs included in this book can be divided into two formats. These formats are based on either computer conferencing or electronic mail. Computer conferencing is a more interactive form of communications in which the instructor and all the students can participate in discussions at the same time. Many courses using this format allow teachers and students to participate in live, online conferences that create a virtual classroom in which some students may be thousands of miles from the instructor.

Electronic mail format, or e-mail, is generally limited to one-way communications that can be conducted at any time of day or night. For example, a student might leave a question for the teacher in the teacher's e-mail mailbox. The following day, the student may find the answer in her or his own mailbox. In some cases, students e-mail their assignments directly into the college's computer, where they are reviewed, scored, and returned to the student with appropriate notations.

Each of the colleges included in the online course and online degree program directories in Part Two of this book has its own protocol concerning the means and times of communications between students and teachers. When you enroll, the school will provide you with complete instructions.

DECIDING WHETHER DISTANCE LEARNING IS RIGHT FOR YOU

Now that you have a better idea of what alternative education is, you will want to know what it will mean to you should you elect to participate in such a program. This knowledge will help you decide whether alternative education is the proper route for you to follow to earn your degree.

The programs described in this book vary in subject, content, learning formats, and costs, but all have in common a strong reliance on the individual as a self-learner. Successful participants must be highly motivated and self-disciplined. In many cases, these programs may take less time and are less costly than traditional college programs, but they can be more demanding in other ways.

This approach to learning is not for everyone; many people need a structured environment in order to engage in college-level learning. A newspaper advertisement once asked readers to select one of the following five goals they wanted to achieve from higher education:

1. Membership in a good fraternity or sorority
2. Lots of great football weekends
3. A nice variety of dates
4. Memories to last a lifetime
5. A job

The ad was for career training conducted by a major aerospace corporation; if you selected number 5, company representatives might be interested in talking to you.

If we use a similar technique for external and nontraditional college degree programs, and you are asked to select the statement that best describes what you require to be a successful learner, the choices might read:

1. A schedule of learning and study that is regulated by the institution or instructor
2. Participation in regular classroom analysis of the subject
3. Close supervision or reinforcement by a professor
4. The ability to regularly discuss the work with classmates
5. General guidance to reach a specified goal

If you selected any of the first four options, you should be extremely cautious about deciding to undertake a course of study in an external degree program. The only characterization that applies to such a program is number 5.

Several years ago, Paula Spier of Antioch University identified the type of individual most likely to succeed in an external degree program when she said Antioch was "looking for autonomous, highly motivated adults, with a quite clear sense of educational goals and their implementation." Does this describe you? Can you clearly identify and state your educational goals?

So before you select one of the external degree programs reviewed in this or any book, you must decide whether you are able to meet the necessary criteria for success.

2 How to Succeed at Independent Study

Some students in both external and traditional programs consider their efforts to earn a degree nothing more than a credit chase—a race to accumulate as many credits as possible by any means available. If you seek to broaden your knowledge and acquire a well-rounded education in your chosen field, earning your degree through alternative methods can be an exciting and rewarding experience.

If your goal is knowledge as well as a degree, you must practice good study habits. How long has it been since you really studied something to learn? Study habits tend to deteriorate when not used.

READING: THE KEY TO LEARNING

All external degree programs, including the online courses and online programs in this book, place strong emphasis on learning through reading. Some schools call this guided reading, directed study, or simply independent reading/study. You are expected to learn quite a bit as a result of an extensive reading program regardless of what the process is called. It is important then to review the methods of study that will help you maximize your learning from all that effort.

Most educators agree that there is no single best way to study; external factors such as time and location influence the experience in varying measures. Many educators agree that there is a most productive way to use a text to learn. The authors of two classic study guides developed their own theories about the most effective method of learning from a book. In *Effective Study,* Francis P. Robinson used what he called the Survey Q3R method. Thomas F. Staton presented his PQRST method in his book *How to Study.* These are the five elements of each method:

Survey Q3R	PQRST
1. Survey	1. Preview
2. Question	2. Question
3. Read	3. Read
4. Recite	4. State
5. Review	5. Test

The basic approach to successful study is common to both methods. Here is how you can make use of it.

1. *Examine the Book.* First, give the book a general examination. This means you should not open it to the first page and immediately begin reading. Develop a feel for the book before studying it. Keeping in mind that your goal is to learn, read through the table of contents. A survey of the chapter titles and chapter descriptions (if any) will help you understand the author's approach to the subject. In some cases, reading the contents will also give you a broad overview of what you will be studying later.

   Next, read the front matter of the book: the preface, introduction, and/or foreword. These sections will usually tell you the purpose, scope, and framework of the book, as well as provide insight into the sources of information the author used and how and why the book was written. The front matter may also compare the book to previous books on the same or similar subjects.

   When you have read the front matter, glance through the index, bibliography, glossary, appendices, and any illustrations and diagrams the book may contain. Finally, if the book includes or is accompanied by a study guide, by all means read it.

2. *Ask Questions.* Frame questions about the text to help yourself better understand the subject. Doing so will also help you to remember longer

what you have read; it is accepted that questions answered leave a more lasting impression than simply reading the same information.

Build questions around chapter titles or subheadings. If a chapter is titled "The Causes of World War I," ask yourself, "What were the causes of World War I?" and then seek the answers while you read the chapter. Question statements in the text and make the author provide answers. If you cannot find an answer, consult some of the sources in the footnotes and/or bibliography. If the question is of sufficient importance, do not stop until you find a satisfactory answer. You may discover information that other readers will miss. As you repeat this technique, you will develop a questioning attitude about everything you read; significant questions will suggest themselves to you more easily as a result. The questioning reader almost always learns more from a text than does the reader who fails to question.

Some textbook authors pose their own questions to the student, usually at the beginning or end of each chapter. Unfortunately, many students disregard this important study aid. If at all possible, consider these questions before reading the chapter, and be sure you are able to answer them when you are finished reading.

3. *Be an Active Reader.* By habit, most people are passive readers. Reading a text to learn something is profoundly different from, say, reading a novel for entertainment. The information in your text must be explored, understood, and remembered. Here are some active reading tips to help you absorb the material:

- Use a see-through felt marker to highlight important or key phrases and words. Be discriminating about what you highlight or you may find that you have emphasized most of the material in the chapter.
- Use the margins as space for writing questions or comments that come to mind while reading. Go back later and seek out the answers or explanations and note the answers in the margins, also.
- Take notes on the major points or concepts expressed in the material. Your notes need not be exhaustive, but they should be descriptive. Note-taking serves two purposes. First, it helps you remember the concepts and important points better than simple reading does. It also gives you a ready reference for review purposes.

4. *Read It Aloud.* When you have finished reading the chapter, go back once more and read aloud the material you previously highlighted along

with the notes you made in the margins. Finally, reread the notes you made on the major points. At first you may feel a bit foolish reading aloud, but you will be surprised how effective this can be in helping you retain important information. Recitation is commonly used in grammar school because it is so productive. Student resistance often prevents use of this method in the higher grades. Forget about feeling foolish. Reading aloud is a good device for learning, so use it, even if it means finding an empty room in which to read.

5. *Review.* After following the first four steps, you should be thoroughly familiar with the subject. Give the highlighted material and your notes one final read. Do not let what you have learned get stale or evaporate before you have a chance to use it.

PROPER PREPARATION FOR EXAMS

Every external degree course will require you to take written examinations. A few external degree programs dictate acceptable scores on entrance examinations, many have comprehensive examinations at some point in the program, and others require a series of examinations throughout the entire program. One thing is virtually certain: If you are going to earn college credits or a degree by traditional or nontraditional methods, you are going to be tested.

Here are some tips that will help you achieve your best performance on practically any test.

1. *Prepare for the Test.* This may sound like an elementary and unnecessary observation, but even many accomplished graduate students procrastinate until they haven't enough time to prepare properly. First, review the material you have studied. Pay careful attention to the points you have highlighted. Invest the time that is really required to review the information until you are as knowledgeable about the subject matter as possible. Try to find out, too, what sorts of questions are going to be asked. Professors are frequently willing to let you know the areas they plan to emphasize in an examination.

2. *Know the Test.* The format of the test is important because it directly relates to your ability to provide correct answers. Some of us are better at expository essay answers than are others, but if you never thor-

oughly mastered that ability, you will want to learn to do so now.

It's true that alternative response, multiple choice, and completion questions also appear on some tests administered to college students, just as are those that require you to match entries in column A with corresponding entries in column B, but you learned how to deal with those many years ago.

3. *Your Physical Preparation.* An examination can be a grueling experience, so be physically prepared. Get plenty of rest during the week prior to the test. Many people find it counterproductive to stay up until the early hours cramming; some then suffer from an information overload that their minds cannot process. Set a reasonable study schedule and keep it. Get enough sleep the night before the test, and arrive at the test site early to give yourself time to relax in an otherwise tense environment.

4. *Taking the Examination.* Once you have prepared yourself mentally and physically for the examination, do not waste that effort by sloppy test-taking practices. Even the most experienced test-taker can profit from following these simple procedures:

- Read all instructions carefully and follow them precisely.
- Quickly review the entire test, noting the relatively easy and difficult parts.
- Unless you are directed to answer the questions sequentially, answer the easier questions first.
- Read each question twice to be sure you completely understand it before answering.
- Do not guess unless the guess is based on something substantial. Many test scoring procedures subtract the number of incorrect answers from the total correct answers to handicap guessers.
- Write legibly. Poor penmanship can cost you the benefit of the doubt if any arises.
- Try to leave enough time to review your answers. Do not rush, but do not waste time either.

SCHEDULING YOUR STUDY TIME

In any endeavor, uncontrolled time can be your worst enemy. You can't save it, you can't recycle it, and once it's lost, it's gone forever. Gaining control of your time is the most important thing you can do to establish a successful study schedule. Remember, not all your time will be spent in front of your computer monitor. Many more hours will be spent studying and preparing for exams than you might expect.

First, identify exactly what you are now doing with your time. It may help to keep a log for a short period. One way to do this is to prepare a list of the major activities that make up your day. Begin with the time you normally awaken and carry it all the way through to the time you normally go to sleep. Be sure the activities you have listed account for the entire day. Transfer these activities to a chart that breaks each day down into increments of one hour or less. You should prepare a chart for each day of the week, because activities differ from one day to the next. Identify those portions of your day that can be sacrificed to your study schedule. If you're like most people, there are few activities you can completely eliminate.

Looking at your activities, you will probably find the first hour committed to essential items: washing, dressing, eating, and so on. The second hour may be spent commuting to work on some form of mass transportation, which offers some opportunity to read assignments. It may mean giving up reading the morning newspaper or playing cards on the train, but you'll know your priorities. I recall a commuter who proudly told everyone who would listen, "I earned my degree on the Long Island Railroad."

For those students who drive their own car to work, and obviously cannot spend their travel time reading, one option is to check the local library to see whether any of the assigned books have been recorded on audio tape. If so, you can listen to the tape while commuting back and forth to work.

Unless you must devote your lunch hour to business associates or business-related matters, you can probably accommodate additional study time then. The ride home also allows some study time. So far, we've identified almost three hours of potential study time in a single day on this chart. Unless you have remarkable powers of concentration, none of this study time is under ideal conditions. The time will at least allow you to familiarize yourself with the reading assignments.

The hour you spend with your children, if you have any, is important to their development and your family life. You should try to avoid asking them to sacrifice their time with you, especially if they are young. If they are teenagers, they will probably be glad you have found something else to do. What is left is the time many people spend watching television. This is probably the best time to convert to productive use.

If your day is typical, then between the time the children go to bed and the time you retire there are three hours of what should be relative calm in which to study. Trying to set aside that much time each night may be unrealistic, but if you can do so for three or four nights each week you should be able to establish a solid study schedule.

It is important not to overestimate the amount of study time you can allow yourself. If there are television programs you really want to watch, delete their broadcast time from your schedule. Be realistic; it will pay off later.

Parents of young children, especially those who stay at home with them, will find it difficult to allocate time for studying. You might try rising an hour earlier, utilizing the children's nap time, or asking a friend to take turns with you babysitting a few afternoons each week.

It will help if you discuss with family members your need to devote yourself to your studies during the periods you've set aside. They are the people most likely to interrupt your work so they must be made to realize the importance of their role. Enlist their cooperation in keeping noise levels down while you are studying. Of course, it's best if you have a quiet separate room in your home that you can use for study.

When planning your study schedule, there are several rules you should follow:

1. *Do Not Overdo It.* Do not plan your study time unrealistically. If you try to force yourself immediately into a grinding study schedule, you may find the entire process unpleasant. This will make it easy to find fault elsewhere when you avoid studying.
2. *Plan for the Times Likely to Be Most Productive.* Studying is basically an individual activity, especially independent study. Plan your study schedule around those times you can be alone.
3. *Do Not Time-Share Study Periods.* Few people can study and listen to music or watch television at the same time. Avoid the impulse to be entertained when you should be learning.
4. *Start with Short Study Periods.* Short study periods are especially important for those people who have been away from school for several years. Disciplining yourself to develop the habit of studying and learning can be similar to beginning an exercise program. You will find it helpful in

the long run if you begin by studying for short periods and then work your way up to longer, more productive study sessions.

When you have fully prepared your study schedule plan, make a concerted effort to live up to it. This may prove to be the most difficult part of your entire program, but it may also be the most important.

Planning your study time to meet your needs and sticking to the plan are actually a plan for success. A good study schedule will provide you with the proper environment and frame of mind for successful independent study.

LEARNING CONTRACTS AND DEGREE PLANS

You already know that most, if not all, of the learning in external and most nontraditional college degree programs is accomplished by the student, independent of direct supervision other than that you receive via your computer. In some cases, this learning takes place through courses specifically developed for this purpose or through faculty-assigned projects that may require extensive research or writing of a thesis or series of essays on preselected subjects or areas of study. Many programs include in their requirements that the student, with the counsel and approval of one or more faculty members, draft a written statement commonly called a learning contract or degree plan.

Although learning contracts and degree plans vary widely from school to school, their purpose is the same: to establish guidelines along which your learning activities will proceed. When the school approves your plan or contract, an agreement has been reached that states that both parties have a clear understanding of exactly what they will be doing during your course of study.

The basic elements of one of these documents are statements of the following:

- Your educational goals
- What you intend to learn
- What methods you will use to acquire that learning
- What resources you will use
- What educational activities you will engage in
- How what you have learned will be tested and evaluated

Some learning contracts are binding on both parties. If you fail to carry out the agreed-on plan, you may be forced to withdraw from the program, forfeiting a portion or all of your tuition, although the majority are not this rigid. If you satisfactorily complete the plan, the school is bound to honor its commitment to award you a degree or a previously specified number of credits toward it. The contract may also include an arbitration clause should a dispute arise over the evaluation or should there be a conflict over the interpretation of some aspect of the agreement.

The resources you use and the activities you engage in will depend on what you want to learn. These may take the form of classes at a nearby college, an internship, volunteer work, a tutorial, a research project, time spent observing and reporting on a certain activity, reading and evaluating any number of previously agreed-on books, analyzing case studies or writing your own, correspondence courses from an accredited institution, recognized proficiency examinations, development of an experiential portfolio based on what knowledge you have acquired in your life, or any of an almost unlimited number and variety of learning activities.

A SAMPLE LEARNING CONTRACT

This example of one form of a learning contract is reprinted with the kind permission of Saint Mary's College, Winona, Minnesota.

I. Personal Data

Name: _____

Permanent Address: _____

Present Address: _____

Present Occupation and Place:_____

II. General Personal and Professional Goals for: (a) This Contract, and (b) Your Degree Program

My goals for this program are (1) to systemize and supplement a diverse but unconnected and theoretically limited knowledge of developmental disabilities caused by deafness and mental retardation; (2) to coordinate this knowledge with specific empirical work in these areas.

This contract will also lay the groundwork for future contracts by addressing the larger issues of (a) the role of language and cognition in development and (b) a theory of health that integrates disability into the concept of the "norm."

III. Specific Education Objectives/Means to Achieve Them/Evaluation of Achievement

On the next page, in outline form, list each objective. Under the objective, list the means you intend to use to achieve it. This could include (1) formal classes, workshops, seminars, institutes, including where taken and number of credits requested; (2) in-service programs, learning experiences, or supervised internships; and (3) independent study with graduate advisor or other professional, including reading list, experiences, papers, film list, discussion topics, and so forth. Again, under each objective, list the means by which you will evaluate whether or not you have achieved your objective.

(SAMPLE OBJECTIVE)

OBJECTIVE 1

I will examine language development in deaf children, incorporating the concepts developed in contract 1.

A. Differences in the language development of deaf and hearing children (pre- and postlingual) will be explored. Sign language grammar and syntax will be compared to that of English. I will acquire fluency in Amesian, the American Sign Language (1,500 words).

B. The role of language in cognition will be investigated. I propose that deafness in itself is not disabling; only as it correlates to social isolation does the deaf person perceive the world differently from his hearing counterpart. The nature of this "social handicapping" will be examined and a conceptual framework developed to describe the psychosocial dynamics that occur between disabled and nondisabled populations.

MEANS

1. I will examine the literature on deafness and psycholinguistics (Noam Chomsky, Hans Furth, etc.).
2. I will interview professionals in the field of deaf education and observe a class for deaf children.
3. I will attend a six-week, two-credit course at Gallaudet College in conversational sign language (36 class-hours).
4. I will produce a case study on one deaf adolescent, which will be structured around the concept of social handicapping developed in part B above.

EVALUATION CRITERIA

A. I will write an evaluation of the reading material and submit the case study.
B. I will be graded on my sign language performance in the Gallaudet course.
C. I will discuss with deaf friends their opinion on the information I've obtained.
D. I will write my own reflections on learning sign language and the effect on me when I am the only hearing person in a group of deaf people.
E. I will consult my special supervisor for this objective: Anne McS. Brahm, M.S., Gallaudet College (Deaf Counseling).

IV. Progress and Evaluation Reports: Additions to Portfolio
A. Self-evaluation and reports to the staff on each specific educational objective.
B. A substantial summary integrating statement.
C. Staff evaluation (to be filed by staff).

I understand and agree to the terms of this contract. I further understand that this contract covers the _____ quarter of my graduate work, which I intend to begin on the _____ day of _____ , 19 _____ and complete on the _____ day of _____ , 19 .

Signed: _____ (Student)   Signed: _____ (Director)

Date: _____   Signed: _____ (Adviser)

Credits: _____

3 Selecting the Right Courses and Degree Program

The decision to engage in study through an online or other nontraditional degree program should be made with the understanding that it requires a genuine commitment to do the necessary work. Before you do that, you must honestly assess your ability to perform successfully in a learning environment that is probably substantially less structured than any you may have encountered in your previous educational experience. Both concerns are real; only you will be the loser if you deceive yourself.

Anyone who looks at one of the courses in this book and thinks, "This looks easy enough," is making a big mistake. These courses are *different* from most traditional courses, but that does not mean they are easier. On the contrary, many people who have been successful in classroom-based courses with a professor regulating their work and peers with whom to discuss the work find courses and programs based on, or making substantial use of, independent study methods considerably more difficult.

SETTING GOALS AND GETTING MOTIVATED

Once you have read the descriptions of the various courses reviewed in this book, you may be asking yourself again why you are considering earning a college degree. Your answer must be formulated in the context of your long-range career and life goals. A college degree may be an impressive credential, but if it is not going to provide additional foundation for your personal and professional growth, you must decide whether you will have the drive to complete courses or a program that may at times be grueling and often solitary.

By their nature and intent, online degree programs are designed to minimize interference with the professional lives of their participants. Independent study projects, research assignments, fieldwork, seminars and classes, and thesis and dissertation preparation all require time from the portion of your life usually devoted to social and family activities. Is your motivation to earn a college degree strong enough to see you through this kind of sacrifice? Will you be able to make your spouse, friends, and relatives understand the importance of reducing their demands on your time? Will you be able to cope with what amounts to a radical change in your life-style? None of this is meant to terrify you, but it is important that you address and answer these questions honestly before you make the commitment to engage in study toward a college degree. The rewards you will reap from possessing a degree must be identifiable and to some extent quantifiable. They must be worth the effort or you will risk the possibility of faltering and ultimate failure.

Students enrolled in online courses generally do not find themselves in the traditional subordinate role vis-à-vis the teacher. It is common for faculty members to relate to most online degree students on an adult level because that is what they usually are. Some students are held in an esteem appropriate to their previously demonstrated success in their chosen professions. A unique respect is accorded those returning to the education process to fine-tune their talents and abilities for professional and personal growth. Despite this, there must still remain an element of the time-honored teacher–student relationship. Many people, especially managers and supervisors, sometimes find it difficult to adjust to their role of student.

If your career goals are within the field in which you now work, you probably already have a good conception of the potential rewards of possessing a college degree. If you plan to use college training and credentials to change fields, take enough time to learn as much as possible about your ultimate goal. Talk to people who work or practice in the field. Analyze the life-styles they lead as a result of their careers, the type of work they perform, and the rewards, benefits, and disadvantages of their careers as they see them. You will find many people surprisingly candid once you have explained the reason for your interest.

Whether your career path is in your present field or you are planning a switch, it is important to know where you are heading, why, and when you can reasonably expect to get there. With all of that resolved, you can begin to develop an action plan to accomplish your career goals that will include your educational goals. You should normally be able to tie the degree you seek directly to the type of work you want to perform. Recall that the schools themselves are looking for adult students "with a quite clear sense of educational goals and their implementation."

One method to help ensure the correct degree concentration for the position you want is to ask those doing the same work what degrees they hold. Go one step farther and ask whether they would seek a different degree concentration as preparation for their present work if they had the opportunity.

While deciding which program to undertake, bear in mind the external pressures you may face. Although they may mean well, family and friends might not always understand your personal goals; their influence can sometimes do more harm than good. All too many people are working in fields that hold little real interest or promise for them because they allowed a relative or friend to cloud their thought processes and turn them in the wrong direction. You may also be influenced by concern about what to do with college credits you may have already earned. Do not succumb to that consideration and apply to a program simply because your previous credits will make earning a degree that much easier and quicker. If it is the wrong degree for your goals, or it will lead you into a career in which you will not be happy, set aside those earlier efforts and start fresh in the program that will help you achieve what will make you happy.

COMMITTING YOUR TIME

The amount of time one must commit to studies depends on a number of factors, which include the structure of the program. Earnest pursuit of a college degree through an online or other nontraditional program can be expected, on average, to require the investment of approximately twenty hours per week in study, research, and related activities. If you skipped over the section "Scheduling Your Study Time," in Chapter 2, you will be wise to go back and read it.

Just as important as scheduling your time is honoring your promise to yourself to actually invest the necessary hours and effort to earn your degree. Examine your life-style and your present commitments. Be sure there are enough hours in your days and weeks to accomplish your degree goal before you apply. This may require serious heart-to-heart conversations with those around you, but better now than under the pressure of misunderstanding or on the brink of failure.

ASSESSING YOUR ABILITY

In an earlier chapter, we defined independent study as any form of formal learning the student accomplishes alone, without a conventional instructor or class environment. The freedom to pace your studies according to your own needs can be one of the most attractive features of most online degree programs. It is also a feature some find a disadvantage. Only you can assess your ability to function well in a relatively unstructured environment.

For the motivated self-disciplined self-starter, independent study offers the opportunity to engage in learning that otherwise might not be possible and to reach a goal that might otherwise be unreachable, a college degree. It permits a student to shape study time around work and family life. It is not uncommon to find adults who are enrolled in nontraditional college courses or external degree programs, such as those described in this book, reading course texts or reviewing assignments while eating lunch, commuting to work and home, or flying across country. This kind of flexibility suits them well, and they find greater pleasure in learning than they might if they were tied to a class schedule. For those with less self-discipline, this type of study can prove disastrous, and the whole process becomes a burden that eventually becomes too heavy to carry.

Some educators are fond of saying that learning is a lifelong experience. This may be true, but most of the learning we do in the course of our lives does not require that we pass a comprehensive examination or write a thesis or project report. Independent study may sound seductively easy, but it isn't. If you lack the discipline required to succeed in an online program you are better advised to find a classroom-based program. Ask yourself the following questions. Your answers will help you evaluate your own ability to function satisfactorily in this type of program.

- What is my motivation for earning a degree?
- Will I make the time available to do the quality of work required?
- Do I have the self-discipline to establish and maintain an adequate study schedule?
- Can I do the work without having an instructor providing regular, almost daily, assistance?
- Can I learn college-level material properly outside the classroom?

SELECTING A COURSE OR PROGRAM

When you have completed your self-assessment, and you are ready to tackle earning a college degree through an online or other nontraditional program, begin by reviewing the degree programs in this book. Bear in mind that the exact title of a degree is sometimes imprecise; the program content and structure are often more important. Carefully read the descriptions of the courses and programs that offer the degree you want in the subject area you have selected for your career and personal development. Assuming more than one external degree program is available in your subject, review the factors that will help you decide which is right for you.

None of the course and program descriptions in this or any other book can be as current as the information the school itself can furnish. Accordingly, after you have used the guidance here to narrow down the field, contact the schools in which you are interested for their online course catalogs, and let the information in them help you make your final selection.

PLACES TO SAVE YOUR CREDITS

Occasionally the question arises, "What if I can't decide on a specific degree program or school but want to continue earning credits through online courses and other nontraditional methods?" The solution is simple—you put your credits in a bank and save them, just as you do your money. Credit banking is the same as money banking, except your credits will not earn interest and grow of their own accord.

Credit banks provide an evaluation and record-keeping service that permits you to accumulate in a single transcript any college-level credits you have earned in the past or plan on earning in the future. If and when you decide to enroll in a degree program, you can have the credit bank forward the school an official transcript of your past work. In some cases, the school may require the submission of transcripts from the original source.

Credit banking is especially useful for individuals who have earned credits from noncollegiate sources such as military training programs or PONSI-approved noncollegiate training and for those who have attended several different colleges or who have taken various proficiency examinations.

For more detailed information on credit banking, including enrollment and credit evaluation fees, contact one or all of the following:

Regents Credit Bank
University of the State of New York
7 Columbia Circle
Albany, NY 12203
(518) 464-8500

Charter Oak State College
Credit Banking
270 Farmington Avenue
Farmington, CT 06032-1934
(203) 677-0076

Thomas Edison State College
Credit Banking
101 West State Street
Trenton, NJ 08608-1176
(609) 984-1150

PART 2

The Electronic College Directories

4 Directory of Web Site Home Pages of North American Colleges and Universities

Colleges and universities throughout the nation are putting themselves online at a rapid rate. To help you locate the newest online college services, such as courses, degree programs, and library access, this chapter provides a directory of the home page locations of those colleges and universities with web sites at the time this book was prepared.

From your home or office computer, you can browse through these home pages and quickly identify those schools that have recently added online courses to their offerings. Be on the lookout for key words that are most likely to lead you to these courses, such as *distance learning, independent study,* and *online programs.*

THE INTERNET, THE WEB, AND YOU

If you are new to the world of the Internet, or if you aren't exactly new to it but aren't quite sure what it is you've been doing, there are a large number of books designed to help you available at any bookstore. Too often though, these tend to be written by "net-nerds," and are weighted down with so much technical information that their actual usefulness to those of us who just want to use the Internet without becoming technical experts is greatly diminished. Two books which you may find helpful in introducing you to the world of the Internet and the World Wide Web without bogging you down are *The Internet for Dummies,* by John R. Levine and Carol Baroudi (IDG Books), and *Internet for Kids,* by Ted Pedersen and Francis Moss (Price Stern Sloan). Don't let the title of the second book deter you from reading it. Although written for children, its simple and direct approach to providing information will prove useful to many adults.

For those of you who just want to plunge ahead, I have included some information that will prove helpful, especially for novices.

First, a quick explanation of the system you will use to contact colleges and universities, and through which you can take courses or even earn a degree. The Internet is an enormous network that connects tens of thou-

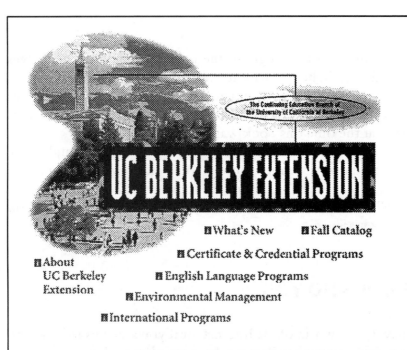

■ What's New   ■ Fall Catalog

■ Certificate & Credential Programs

■ About
UC Berkeley   ■ English Language Programs
Extension
■ Environmental Management

■ International Programs

What's New	Fall Catalog	Certificate & Credential Programs
English Language Programs	Environmental Management	International Programs
About UC Berkeley Extension	UC Berkeley Home Page

Send your comments and suggestions to pmd@unx.berkeley.edu

Last updated 27 Aug 1996

sands of other networks together, making them and the information they contain accessible to virtually anyone with a computer. The World Wide Web is a delivery system that makes it easy for anyone equipped with what is called a Web browser to travel or navigate through the Internet looking for the information they need. Web browser software is usually provided by companies that sell access to the Internet. The most popular of these companies are America Online and CompuServe, although there are dozens of others from which to choose. Subscribing to one of these services entitles you to access the Internet, in addition to other services provided by the company. The cost of a subscription varies from one service to another and may be affected by how your local telephone company bills for calls. Examples of Web browser software include Web Crawler (provided by American Online), Microsoft Explorer (provided by the Microsoft Network), and the popular Netscape.

Now, let's take a look at those all important addresses that in no way resemble the addresses we are all used to using in the world beyond computers. The addresses below and those in the rest of this book all begin with the letters "http." This stands for *hypertext transfer protocol.* Hypertext is a system of links that connect pieces of related information together even though they may be from different sources. In many addresses you'll also see "www," which stands for *World Wide Web.* All addresses for colleges and other educational institutions end with "edu," which means simply that the address is that of an educational institution. The remainder of most of the addresses in the following directory are pretty much self-explanatory. For example, Albertson College of Idaho is identified in its address as *acofi.* While others may be a bit more complex, the basic approach is the same.

The addresses in this directory are the home pages for each college and university. A home page is a sort of table of contents for the information each institution has decided to include in its online service. Beginning at the home page you can move through a series of pages that might include listings of courses, directions to the school, e-mail addresses for faculty members, and a wealth of other data.

Abilene Christian University, Abilene, TX
    http://cteserver.acu.edu/
Agnes Scott College, Decatur, GA
    http://www.scottlan.edu/
Albert Einstein College of Medicine, Bronx, NY
    http://www.aecom.yu.edu/

Albertson College of Idaho, Caldwell, ID
   http://www.acofi.edu/
Albion College, Albion, MI
   http://www.albion.edu/
Alderson-Broaddus College, Philippi, WV
   http://www.mountain.net/ab/
Alfred University, Alfred, NY
   http://www.alfred.edu/
Allentown College, Allentown, PA
   http://www.allencol.edu/
Amherst College, Amherst, MA
   http://www.amherst.edu/start.html
Andrews University, Berrien Springs, MI
   http://www.cs.andrews.edu/index.html
Angelo State University, San Angelo, TX
   http://www.angelo.edu/
Antioch College, Yellow Springs, OH
   http://college.antioch.edu/
Appalachian State University, Boone, NC
   http://www.acs.appstate.edu/
Arizona State University, Tempe, AZ
   http://info.asu.edu/
Assumption College, Worcester, MA
   http://www.assumption.edu:80/
Auburn University, Auburn, AL
   http://mallard.duc.auburn.edu/
Augsburg College, Minneapolis, MN
   http://www.augsburg.edu/
Augustana College, Rock Island, IL
   http://www.augustana.edu/
Austin College, Sherman, TX
   http://www.austinc.edu/
Azusa Pacific University, Azusa, CA
   http://apu.edu/
Baker University, Baldwin City, KS
   http://www.bakeru.edu/
Ball State University, Muncie, IN
   http://www.bsu.edu/
Bard College, Annondale-on-Hudson, NY
   http://www.bard.edu/

Bates College, Lewiston, ME
  http://abacus.bates.edu/
Baylor College of Medicine, Waco, TX
  http://www.bcm.tmc.edu/
Baylor University, Waco, TX
  http://www.baylor.edu/
Beaver College
  http://www.beaver.edu/
Belmont University, Nashville, TN
  http://acklen.belmont.edu/
Beloit College, Beloit, WI
  http://stu.beloit.edu/
Berea College, Berea, KY
  http://www.berea.edu/
Bethany College, Bethany, MD
  http://info.bethany.wvnet.edu/
Bethel College, Newton, KS
  http://www.bethelks.edu/
Bethel College and Seminary, St. Paul, MN
  http://www.bethel.edu/
Binghamton University, Binghamton, NY
  http://www.binghamton.edu/
Biola University, La Mirada, CA
  http://www.biola.edu/
Blackburn College, Calinville, IL
  http://www.mcs.net/-kwplace/bc.htm
Bloomsburg University, Bloomsburg, PA
  http://www.bloomu.edu/
Boise State University, Boise, ID
  http://www.idbsu.edu/
Boston College, Chestnut Hill, MA
  http://infoeagle.bc.edu/
Boston University, Boston, MA
  http://web.bu.edu/
Bowdoin College, Brunswick, ME
  http://www.bowdoin.edu/
Bowling Green State University, Bowling Green, OH
  http://www.bgsu.edu/
Bradley University, Peoria, IL
  http://www.bradley.edu/

Brandeis University, Waltham, MA
http://www.brandeis.edu/
Bridgewater College, Bridgewater, VA
http://www.bridgewater.edu/
Brigham Young University, Provo, UT
http://www.byu.edu/
Brown University, Providence, RI
http://www.brown.edu/
Bryn Mawr College, Bryn Mawr, PA
http://www.brynmawr.edu/college/
Bucknell University, Lewisburg, PA
http://www.bucknell.edu/
Buena Vista University, Storm Lake, IA
http://www.bvu.edu/
Butler University, Indianapolis, IN
http://www.butler.edu/
California College for Health Sciences, National City, CA
http://www.cchs.edu/
California Institute of Technology, Pasadena, CA
http://www.caltech.edu/
California Institute of the Arts, Valencia, CA
http://www.calarts.edu/
California Lutheran University, Thousand Oaks, CA
http://robles.callutheran.edu/
California State Polytechnic University, Pomona, CA
http://www.csupomona.edu/welcome.html
California State Polytechnic University, San Luis Obispo, CA
http://www.calpoly.edu/
California State University, Chico, CA
http://www.csuchico.edu/
California State University, Fresno, CA
http://www.csufresno.edu/
California State University, Fullerton, CA
http://www.fullerton.edu/
California State University, Hayward, CA
http://www.mcs.csuhayward.edu/
California State University, Long Beach, CA
http://www.csulb.edu/
California State University, Los Angeles, CA
http://www.calstatela.edu/

California State University, Northridge, CA
  http://www.csun.edu/
California State University, Sacramento, CA
  http://www.csus.edu/
California State University, San Bernardino, CA
  http://www.csusb.edu/
California State University, San Marcos, CA
  http://coyote.csusm.edu/
California State University, Stanislaus, CA
  http://lead.csustan.edu/
Calvin College, Grand Rapids, MI
  http://www.calvin.edu/
Carleton College, Northfield, MN
  http://www.carleton.edu/
Carnegie Mellon University, Pittsburgh, PA
  http://www.cmu.edu/
Carroll College, Helena, MT
  http://carroll1.cc.edu/
Case Western Reserve University, Cleveland, OH
  http://www.cwru.edu/
Cedarville College, Cedarville, OH
  http://www.cedarville.edu/
Centenary College of Louisiana, Shreveport, LA
  http://alpha.centenary.edu/
Central Connecticut State University, New Britain, CT
  http://neal.ctstateu.edu/home.html
Central Michigan University, Mt. Pleasant, MI
  http://www.cmich.edu/
Central Missouri State University, Warrensburg, MO
  http://cmsuvmb.cmsu.edu/
Central Washington University, Ellensburg, WA
  http://www.cwu.edu/
Centre College, Danville, KY
  http://www.centre.edu/
Cerritos College, Norwalk, CA
  http://www.cerritor.edu/
Chapman University, Orange, CA
  http://www.chapman.edu/
Chicago–Kent College of Law, Chicago, IL
  http://www.kentlaw.edu/

Christian Brothers University, Memphis, TN
    http://www.cbu.edu/
Christopher Newport University, Newport News, VA
    http://www.pcs.cnu.edu/
City University, Seattle, WA
    http://www.cityu.edu/inroads/welcome.htm
City University of New York, New York, NY
    http://www.cuny.edu/
Clark University, Worcester, MA
    http://www.clarku.edu/
Clemson University, Clemson, SC
    http://www.clemson.edu/home.html
Cleveland State University, Cleveland, OH
    http://www.csuohio.edu/
Coe College, Cedar Rapids, IA
    http://www.coe.edu/
Colgate University, Hamilton, NY
    http://cs.colgate.edu/
College of Aeronautics, Flushing, NY
    http://www.mordor.com/coa/coa.html
College of Charleston, Charleston, SC
    http://www.cs.cofc.edu/
College of Eastern Utah, Price, UT
    http://www.ceu.edu/
College of St. Benedict, St. Joseph, MN
    http://www.csbsju.edu/
College of St. Scholastica, Duluth, MN
    http://www.css.edu/
College of the Holy Cross, Worcester, MA
    http://www.holycross.edu/
College of William and Mary, Williamsburg, VA
    http://www.wm.edu/
Colorado College, Colorado Springs, CO
    http://www.cc.colorado.edu/
Colorado School of Mines, Golden, CO
    http://gn.mines.colorado.edu:80/
Colorado State University, Fort Collins, CO
    http://www.colostate.edu/
Columbia College, Chicago, IL
    http://www.colum.edu/

Columbia University, New York, NY
  http://www.columbia.edu/
Concordia College, Ann Arbor, MI
  http://www.cuis.edu/www/cus/cumi.html
Concordia College, Austin, TX
  http://www.cuis.edu/www/cus/cutx.html
Concordia College, Bronxville, NY
  http://www.cuis.edu/www/cus/cuny.html
Concordia College, Moorhead, MN
  http://www.cord.edu/
Concordia College, Portland, OR
  http://www.cuis.edu/www/cus/cuor.html
Concordia College, Selma, AL
  http://www.cuis.edu/www/cus/cual.html
Concordia College, Seward, NE
  http://www.cuis.edu/www/cus/cunb.html
Concordia College, St. Paul, MN
  http://www.cuis.edu/www/cus/cumn.html
Concordia University, Irvine, CA
  http://www.cuis.edu/www/cus/cuca.html
Concordia University, Mequon, WI
  http://www.cuis.edu/www/cus/cuws.html
Concordia University, River Forest, IL
  http://www.cuis.edu/www/curf/home.html
Connecticut College, New London, CT
  http://camel.conncoll.edu/
Cornell University, Ithaca, NY
  http://www.cornell.edu/
Cornerstone College, Grand Rapids, MI
  http://www.grfn.org/~cstone/
Creighton University, Omaha, NE
  http://bluejay.creighton.edu/
Dakota State University, Madison, SD
  http://www.dsu.edu/
Dana College, Buffalo, NY
  http://www.dana.edu/
Dartmouth College, Hanover, NH
  http://www.dartmouth.edu/
Denison University, Granville, OH
  http://louie.cc.denison.edu/

CITY UNIVERSITY

The world is our campus.

Welcome to City University EDROADS
(Education Resource and Online Academic Degree System)
Our Web site offers information about the university and is a vehicle for
students to complete select courses via the Internet.
Browse through our Web site and become familiar with
City University and its program offerings.
Please note that some areas are accessible only to
enrolled students.

F A Q | CU EGYPT | TEXT

Choose this for a textual representation of this page.

City University

The world is our campus

EDROADS

Welcome to City University EDROADS (Education Resource and Online Academic Degree System). Our Web site offers information about the university and is a vehicle for students to complete select courses via the Internet. This Web site promises to be highly interactive, from application and registration through completion of course work and communication with faculty, advisors and other students. Browse through our Web site and become familiar with City University and its program offerings. Please note that some areas are accessible only to enrolled students. If you have suggestions for better serving your information needs, please click here.

- What's New at City U
- Information, Program Offerings, Application
- Registration for Online Programs
- E-mail and Online Classrooms
- Student Lounge

Choose this for a graphical representation of this page.
FAQ:Frequently Asked Questions

DePaul University, Chicago, IL
http://www.depaul.edu/
Diablo Valley College, Pleasant Hill, CA
http://www.dvc.edu/
Dixie College, St. George, UT
http://sci.dixie.edu/
Dordt College, Sioux Center, IA
http://www.dordt.edu:7000/
Drake University, Des Moines, IA
http://www.drake.edu/default.html
Drew University, Department of Academic Technology, Madison, NY
http://tarzan.drew.edu/athome.html

Drexel University, Philadelphia, PA
http://www.drexel.edu/
Duke University, Durham, NC
http://www.duke.edu/
Duquesne University, Pittsburgh, PA
http://www.duq.edu/
Earlham College, Richmond, IN
http://www.admis.earlham.edu/earlham.html
East Carolina University, Greenville, NC
http://ecuvax.cis.ecu.edu/
East Central University, Ada, OK
http://student.ecok.edu/
East Stroudsburg State University, East Stroudsburg, PA
http://www.esu.edu/
East Tennessee State University, Johnson City, TN
http://www.etsu.east-tenn-st.edu/
East Texas State University, Commerce, TX
http://www.etsu.edu/
Eastern Illinois University, Charleston, IL
http://www.eiu.edu/
Eastern Michigan University, Ypsilanti, MI
http://www.emich.edu/
Eastern New Mexico University, Roswell, NM
http://www.enmu.edu/
Eastern Oregon State College, LaGrande, OR
http://www.eosc.osshe.edu/
Eastern Washington University, Cheney, WA
http://www.ewu.edu/
Edinboro University of Pennsylvania, Edinboro, PA
http://www.edinboro.edu/
Embry-Riddle Aeronautical University, Daytona Beach, FL
http://www.db.erau.edu/
Emmanuel College, Boston, MA
http://www.emmanuel.edu/
Emory University, Atlanta, GA
http://www.cc.emory.edu/welcome.html
Emporia State University, Emporia, KS
http://www.emporia.edu/index.html
Fairfield University, Fairfield, CT
http://192.160.243.26/

Fayetteville State University, Fayetteville, NC
   http://www.fsufay.edu/
Ferris State University, Big Rapids, MI
   http://about.ferris.edu/
Fisk University, Nashville, TN
   http://www.fisk.edu/
Florida A&M University, Tallahassee, FL
   http://www.famu.edu:80/~jippolit/FAMU__html/
      html__s/FAMU__top.html
Florida Atlantic University, Boca Raton, FL
   http://www.fau.edu/
Florida Institute of Technology, Melbourne, FL
   http://www.fit.edu/
Florida International University, Miami, FL
   http://nomad.fiu.edu/
Florida State University, Tallahassee, FL
   http://www.fsu.edu/
Fort Hays State University, Fort Hays, KS
   http://fhsuvm.fhsu.edu/
Franklin and Marshall College, Lancaster, PA
   http://www.fandm.edu/
Fullerton College, Fullerton, CA
   http://www.fullcoll.edu/
Furman University, Greenville, SC
   http://www.furman.edu/
Gallaudet University, Washington, DC
   http://www.gallaudet.edu/
Gannon University, Erie, PA
   http://www.gannon.edu/
George Mason University, Fairfax, VA
   http://www.gmu.edu/
George Washington University, Washington, DC
   http://gwis.circ.gwu.edu/
Georgia Institute of Technology, Atlanta, GA
   http://www.gatech.edu/
Georgia Southern University, Statesboro, GA
   http://www.gasou.edu/
Georgia State University, Atlanta, GA
   http://www.gsu.edu/

Gettysburg College, Gettysburg, PA
http://www.gettysburg.edu/

GMI Engineering & Management Institute, Flint, MI
http://www.gmi.edu/

Gonzaga University, Spokane, WA
http://www.gonzaga.edu/

Goshen College, Goshen, IN
http://www.goshen.edu/

Goucher College, Towson, MD
http://www.goucher.edu/

Governors State University, University Park, IL
http://www.bgu.edu/

Graceland College, Lamoni, IA
http://www.graceland.edu/

Grand Valley State University, Allendale, MI
http://www.gvsu.edu/

Grinnell College, Department of Mathematics and Computer Science, Grinnell, IA
http://www.math.grin.edu/

Gustavus Adolphus College, St. Peter, MN
http://www.gac.edu/

Hahnemann University, Philadelphia, PA
http://www.hahnemann.edu/

Hamilton College, Clinton, NY
http://www.hamilton.edu/

Hamline University, St. Paul, MN
http://www.hamline.edu/

Hampden-Sydney College, Hampden-Sydney, VA
http://lion.hsc.edu/

Hampshire College, Amherst, MA
http://www.hampshire.edu/

Hampton University, Hampton, VA
http://www.cs.hamptonu.edu/

Hanover College, Hanover, IN
http://www.hanover.edu/

Harding University, Searcy, AR
http://www.harding.edu/

Hartwick College, Oneonta, NY
http://www.hartwick.edu/

Harvard University, Cambridge, MA
http://www.harvard.edu/
Harvey Mudd College, Claremont, CA
http://www.hmc.edu/
Haverford College, Haverford, PA
http://www.haverford.edu/
Heidelberg College, Tiffin, OH
http://www.heidelberg.edu/
Hendrix College, Conway, AR
http://192.131.98.11/
Hillsdale College, Hillsdale, MI
http://www.hillsdale.edu/
Hiram College, Hiram, OH
http://www.hiram.edu/
Hobart and William Smith Colleges, Geneva, NY
http://hws3.hws.edu:9000/
Hofstra University, Hempstead, NY
http://www.hofstra.edu/
Hope College, Holland, MI
http://www.hope.edu/
Howard University, Washington, DC
http://www.howard.edu/
Humboldt State University, Arcata, CA
http://rocky.humboldt.edu/
Huntington College, Huntington, IN
http://www.huntcol.edu/
Idaho State University, Pocatello, ID
http://www.idu.edu/
Illinois Institute of Technology, Chicago, IL
http://www.iit.edu/
Illinois State University, Normal, IL
http://www.ilstu.edu/
Incarnate Word College, San Antonio, TX
http://www.iwctx.edu/
Indiana Institute of Technology, Ft. Wayne, IN
http://www.indtech.edu/
Indiana State University, Terre Haute, IN
http://www.indstate.edu/
Indiana University, Bloomington, IN
http://www.indiana.edu/

Indiana University of Pennsylvania, Indiana, PA
http://www.lib.iup.edu/
Indiana University Purdue University, Indianapolis, IN
http://indyunix.iupui.edu/
International School of Information Management, Denver, CO
http://www.isim.edu/
Iowa State University, Ames, IA
http://www.iastate.edu/
Ithaca College, Ithaca, NY
http://www.ithaca.edu/
Jacksonville State University, Jacksonville, AL
http://jsucc.jsu.edu/home.html
Jacksonville University, Jacksonville, FL
http://junix.ju.edu/
James Madison University, Harrisonburg, VA
http://www.jmu.edu/
Johnson C. Smith University, Charlotte, NC
http://www.jcsu.edu/index.html
Jones College, Jacksonville, FL
http://www.jones.edu/
Kalamazoo College, Kalamazoo, MI
http://www.kzoo.edu/
Kansas State University, Manhattan, KS
http://www.dce.ksu.edu/
Keene State College, Keene, NH
http://kilburn.keene.edu/
Kent State University, Kent, OH
http://www.kent.edu/
Kenyon College, Gambier, OH
http://www.kenyon.edu/
Kutztown University of Pennsylvania, Kutztown, PA
http://www.kutztown.edu/
La Sierra University, La Sierra, CA
http://www.lasierra.edu/
LaFayette College, Easton, PA
http://www.lafayette.edu/
LaGrange College, LaGrange, GA
http://www.lgc.peachnet.edu/
Lake Forest College, Lake Forest, IL
http://www.lfc.edu/

Lake Superior State University, Sault Ste. Marie, MI
http://www.lssu.edu/
Lamar University, Beaumont, TX
http://www.lamar.edu/
Lasalle University, Philadelphia, PA
http://www.lasalle.edu/
Lawrence University, Appleton, WI
http://www.lawrence.edu/
Lehigh University, Bethlehem, PA
http://www.lehigh.edu/
Lewis & Clark College, Portland, OR
http://www.lclark.edu/
Liberty University, Lynchburg, VA
http://www.liberty.edu/
Linfield College, McMinnville, OR
http://www.linfield.edu/
Lock Haven University, Lock Haven, PA
http://www.lhup.edu/
Louisiana College, Pineville, LA
http://www.lacollege.edu/
Louisiana State University at Baton Rouge, Baton Rouge, LA
http://unix1.sncc.lsu.edu/
Louisiana Tech University, Ruston, LA
http://aurora.latech.edu/
Loyola College, Baltimore, MD
http://www.loyola.edu/
Loyola Marymount University, Los Angeles, CA
http://www.lmu.edu/
Loyola University, Chicago, IL
http://www.luc.edu/
Lycoming College, Williamsport, PA
http://www.lycoming.edu/
Macalester College, St. Paul, MN
http://www.macalstr.edu/
Mankato State University, Mankato, MN
http://www.mankato.msus.edu/
Marist College, Poughkeepsie, NY
http://www.marist.edu/
Marlboro College, Marlboro, VT
http://www.marlboro.edu/

Marquette University, Milwaukee, WI
http://www.mu.edu/
Marshall University, Huntington, WV
http://www.marshall.edu/
Mary Washington College, Fredericksburg, VA
http://www.mwc.edu/
Maryland Institute, College of Art, Baltimore, MD
http://www.mica.edu/
Massachusetts Institute of Technology, Cambridge, MA
http://web.mit.edu/
Massachusetts Maritime Academy, Buzzards Bay, MA
http://www.mma.mass.edu/mma.html
McNeese State University, Lake Charles, LA
http://www.mcneese.edu/
Medical College of Georgia, Augusta, GA
http://www.mcg.edu/
Medical College of Ohio, Toledo, OH
http://www.mco.edu/
Medical College of Wisconsin, Milwaukee, WI
http://www.mcw.edu/
Medical University of South Carolina, Charleston, SC
http://www.radonc.musc.edu/
Mercer University, Atlanta, GA
http://www.mercer.peachnet.edu/
Mercyhurst College, Erie, PA
http://utopia.mercy.edu/
Meredith College, Raleigh, NC
http://www.meredith.edu/meredith/
Messiah College, Grantham, PA
http://www.messiah.edu/
Metropolitan State College of Denver, Denver, CO
http://www.mscd.edu/
Metropolitan State University, St. Paul, MN
http://www.metro.msus.edu/
Miami University of Ohio, Oxford, OH
http://www.muohio.edu/
Michigan State University, East Lansing, MI
http://www.msu.edu/
Michigan Technological University, Houghton, MI
http://www.mtu.edu/

Middle Tennessee State University, Murfreesboro, TN
  http://www.mtsu.edu/
Middlebury College, Middlebury, VT
  http://www.middlebury.edu/
Midwestern State University, Wichita Falls, TX
  http://www.mwsu.edu/
Millersville University, Millersville, PA
  http://marauder.millersv.edu/
Millsaps College, Jackson, MS
  http://www.millsaps.edu/
Milwaukee School of Engineering, Milwaukee, WI
  http://www.msoe.edu/
Mississippi College, Clinton, MS
  http://www.mc.edu/
Mississippi State University, Mississippi State, MS
  http://www.msstate.edu/
Missouri Western State College, St. Joseph, MO
  http://www.mwsc.edu/
Monmouth College, West Long Branch, NJ
  http://www.monmouth.edu/
Montana State University, Bozeman, MT
  http://www.montana.edu/
Montana State University, North Havre, MT
  http://cis.nmclites.edu/
Montclair State University, Montclair, MT
  http://www.montclair.edu/
Monterey Institute of International Studies, Monterey, CA
  http://www.milis.edu/
Moravian College, Bethlehem, PA
  http://www.moravian.edu/
Mount Holyoke College, South Hadley, MA
  http://www.mtholyoke.edu/
Mount Union College, Alliance, OH
  http://www.muc.edu/default.html
Muskingum College, New Concord, OH
  http://www.muskingum.edu/
National Technological University, Fort Collins, CO
  http://www.ntu.edu/
National University, San Diego, CA
  http://numic.nu.edu/

New England Culinary Institute, Montpelier, VT
  http://www.neculinary.com/neci/welcome.htm
New Jersey Institute of Technology, Newark, NJ
  http://www.njit.edu/
New Mexico Institute of Mining and Technology, Socorro, NM
  http://www.nmt.edu/
New Mexico State University, Alamogordo, NM
  http://www.nmsu.edu/
New School for Social Research, New York, NY
  http://dialnsa.edu/home.html
New York Institute of Technology, Central Islip, NY
  http://www.nyit.edu/olc/
New York University, New York, NY
  http://www.nyu.edu/
Nicholls State University, Thibodaux, LA
  http://server.nich.edu/
North Carolina Agricultural and Technical University, Greensboro, NC
  http://www.ncsu.edu/
North Central Bible College, Minneapolis, MN
  http://www.ncbc.edu/
North Dakota State University, Fargo, ND
  http://toons.cc.ndsu.nodak.edu/ndsu/home.html
North Dakota University System, Fargo, ND
  http://www.nodak.edu/
Northeast Louisiana University, Monroe, LA
  http://www.nlu.edu/
Northeast Missouri State University, Kirksville, MO
  http://www.nemostate.edu/
Northeastern State University, Tahlequah, OK
  http://www.nsuok.edu/
Northern Arizona University, Flagstaff, AZ
  http://www.nau.edu/
Northern Illinois University, DeKalb, IL
  http://www.niu.edu/
Northern Michigan University, Marquette, MI
  http://www-ais.acs.nmu.edu/
Northwest Nazarene College, Nampa, ID
  http://www.nnc.edu/homepage.html
Northwestern College, Orange City, IA
  http://solomon.nwciowa.edu/

Northwestern Michigan College, Traverse City, MI
  http://leo.nmc.edu/
Northwestern State University, Natchitoches, LA
  http://server.nsula.edu/
Northwestern University, Evanston, IL
  http://www.acns.nwu.edu/
Nova Southeastern University, Ft. Lauderdale, FL
  http://alpha.acast.nova.edu/start.html
Oakland University, Rochester, MI
  http://www.acs.oakland.edu/
Oberlin College, Oberlin, OH
  http://www.oberlin.edu/
Occidental College, Los Angeles, CA
  http://www.oxy.edu/
Ohio Northern University, Ada, OH
  http://www.onu.edu/
Ohio University, Athens, OH
  http://www.ohiou.edu/
Ontario Institute for Studies in Education, Toronto, Ontario, Canada
  http://www.oise.on.ca/
Pacific Lutheran University, Tacoma, WA
  http://www.plu.edu/
Raritan Valley Community College, North Branch, NJ
  http://raritanval.edu/
Rochester Institute of Technology, Rochester, NY
  http://www.rit.edu/
San Jose State University Continuing Education, San Jose, CA
  http://conted.sjsu.edu/
School of Education–Nagoya University
  http://www.educa.nagoya-u.ac.jp/index-e.html
School of Graduate Studies and Continuing Education, Hartford, CT
  http://www.scsu-sc.ctstateu.edu/grad/
Seattle Pacific University Division of Continuing Education, Seattle, WA
  http://paul.spu.edu/dcs/
Southern Maine Technical College, South Portland, ME
  http://ctech.smtc.mtcs.tec.me.us/
Thomas Edison State College, Trenton, NJ
  http://www.tesc.edu/
U.S. Department of Agriculture–Graduate School
  http://grad.usda.gov/corres/corpro.html

Welcome to Our Home Page

| Help Index | | Glossary of Terms |

 Best listened to using **pwWebSpeak**

Welcome to **Thomas Edison State College!** A national leader in distance education, Thomas Edison enables adult learners to complete baccalaureate and associate degrees wherever they live and work. The College's first graduate degree, the Master of Science in Management, accepted its first students in January 1996. At Thomas Edison, students in any state or nation can earn credit for college-level knowledge acquired outside the classroom. There are no residency requirements. Browse through our pages to discover who we are and what we do.

About Thomas Edison State College

 Learn about the educational philosophy of the College, review our mission statement, read a message from our President, meet our boards (Trustees, Directors, Alumni), consulting faculty and staff, learn about our policies and gather other general informaton about the College.

What's New !!!

 Check here for the latest and greatest about Thomas Edison State College. Visit us frequently to see changes to our Web site, announcements, course information, news releases, and other bright ideas from the nation's premier distance learning institution.

Programs of Study

One of "the brighter stars of higher learning" *(New York Times)*, Thomas Edison offers 119 areas of study leading to 11 bachelor and associate degrees, and a Master of Science in Management, as well as a wide range of nondegree and certificate programs. We welcome students of all ages and backgrounds, in the U.S., abroad, and in the military. **New Jersey residents:** check out our innovative degree completion opportunity with the state's county colleges.

Distance & Independent Adult Learning

101 West State Street
Trenton, NJ 08608-1176

Last updated: 5th December, 1995

| Guided Study | Computer Classroom | Contract Learning |

| College Home Page | | CALL Network | | Help Index | | Course Catalog |

 Distance and independent education describes a collection of approaches to learning which take place outside the traditional college classroom. These approaches have proven most successful with well-motivated, self-disciplined individuals who enjoy learning independently.

Thomas Edison State College's Center for Distance & Independent Adult Learning (DIAL) currently offers three delivery modes for courses:

- Guided Study courses, which are primarily print-based, many with video or audio support;

- On-Line Computer Classroom courses, which utilize computer communications to link distance learners with each other and faculty; and

- Contract Learning courses, that allow students to work independently with faculty to earn credit for courses not readily available in established distance and independent learning formats.

Each is described in detail in the corresponding section of this information. Courses offered in each delivery format are also listed in corresponding sections in the DIAL Course Registration Bulletin. You may request a copy of the Bulletin from the DIAL office by calling (609)292-6317 or follow the link to our **Course Catalog** to search for the information you need. DIAL reserves the right to add or withdraw courses without prior notice.

Each course offered through the Distance & Independent Adult Learning DIAL program is the result of a collaborative process involving faculty from many outstanding institutions and is designed to allow you to learn on your own. Faculty mentors are assigned to specific courses based on their academic experience, current teaching experience and commitment to adult education. Because you do not attend classes or lectures, in-depth reading is central to most courses. The intensive nature of courses allows you to gain a thorough knowledge of the areas you choose to study. The 6- and 9-credit courses are respectively equivalent to taking two or three courses during a semester; the advantage is that your study will be concentrated on a single subject, thus focusing your efforts.

All DIAL courses require that you take proctored examinations. You may schedule your examinations on specified dates at Thomas Edison State College or at one of four designated official New Jersey test sites. If these locations are inconvenient to you, you may take your examinations at an approved site close to where you live or work. You are responsible for paying any proctor fees incurred.

If you are new to distance and independent learning, you should strongly consider purchasing The Good Study Guide by Andrew Northedge, which is considered an excellent resource for making the most of your study time. You can order a copy from Specialty Books at (800) 466-1365 or from MBS

University of California, Davis, CA
http://www-unex.ucdavis.edu/
University of California, Irvine, CA
http://www.unex.uci.edu/~unex/
University of California Extension, Berkeley, CA
http://www-cmil.unex.berkeley.edu/
University of Georgia, Athens, GA
http://www.gactr.uga.edu/
University of Idaho, Moscow, ID
http://www.uidaho.edu/evo/
University of Illinois at Urbana–Champaign, Urbana, IL
http://www.extramural.uiuc.edu/
University of Iowa College of Education, Iowa City, IA
http://www.uiowa.edu/~ccp/
University of Kansas, Lawrence, KS
http://www.sped.ukans.edu:80/spedadmin/welcome.html
University of Michigan, Ann Arbor, MI
http://ics.soe.umich.edu/
University of Minnesota, Minneapolis, MN
http://www.cee.umn.edu/dis/
University of Missouri, Columbia, MO
http://indepstudy.ext.missouri.edu/
University of Nebraska, Lincoln, NE
http://www.unl.edu/
University of North Dakota, Grand Forks, ND
http://www.nodak.edu/
University of Oklahoma, Norman, OK
http://tel.occe.uoknor.edu/
University of Santa Cruz's Online Catalog, Santa Cruz, CA
http://www.ucsc.edu/unex/
University of Tennessee Continuing Education, Chattanooga, TN
http://web.ce.utk.edu/
University of Texas, Austin, TX
http://www.utexas.edu/depts/eimc/
University of Utah, Salt Lake City, UT
http://www.dce.utah.edu/
University of Virginia, Charlottesville, VA
http://www.virginia.edu/
University of Virginia Education Library, Charlottesville, VA
http://curry.edschool.virginia.edu/curry/resources

University of Washington, Seattle, WA
  http://weber.u.washington.edu/~instudy/
University of Winnipeg, Division of Continuing Education, Winnipeg, Canada
  http://www.coned.uwinnipeg.ca/
University of Wisconsin, Madison, WI
  http://www.wisc.edu/

5 Directory of Undergraduate and Graduate College Courses Available Online

The college courses included in this chapter's directory are all available online. Although most are 100 percent online, some may have components requiring students to take part in brief seminars or other activities but, for the most part, are conducted online. Some of these courses are totally interactive, whereas others are based on e-mail communications. Of course, a guide such as this can only be as current as the date it is published, whereas college and university catalogs are published at all times of the year. Therefore, once you have found a course that appeals to you or meets your requirements, contact the school for its latest brochure or catalog.

Unless otherwise identified, all courses listed in the following directory are offered by institutions that are accredited by the most widely recognized accrediting associations, which are in turn recognized by either the U.S. Department of Education or the Council on Recognition of Postsecondary Accreditation or both. Accreditation is a vital factor if you are planning on using the credits earned from online courses toward earning a degree at an accredited college or university. Accreditation is less important if you plan on taking courses for self-enrichment or simply for your own pleasure.

To help you locate the course or courses you want, an easy-to-use college course locator is provided. Before you begin reviewing individual courses, you should read through the entire list of courses in the locator. Often, different schools use different terminology when identifying their courses, so you should acquaint yourself with all of the courses available online before focusing on specific ones.

THE EASY-TO-USE ONLINE COLLEGE COURSE LOCATOR

Arranged in alphabetical order by subject, the following list identifies the online courses available in each subject category and the institutions offering them. The letter U following a course title indicates that the course carries undergraduate credit, which most of these courses do. The letter G means the course is offered for graduate credit. Courses followed by an N are offered on a noncredit basis only. Most of these courses can be taken as noncredit by individuals seeking to improve their knowledge but not interested in pursuing a degree.

Following the locator, all colleges are listed in alphabetical order, with all important data grouped immediately following the institution's name. Information on the individual courses offered by each college is then grouped by subject category, the same as in the locator.

Accounting
  Accounting I, University of Missouri, U
  Accounting II, University of Missouri, U
  Fundamentals of Managerial Accounting, University of Washington, U
  Governmental Accounting, University of California Extension, U
Afro-American/African Studies
  Introduction to African Literature, University of Minnesota, U
Agriculture
  Introduction to Computers in Agriculture, Southern Illinois
    University, U
American Indian Studies
  American Indian History I, University of Minnesota, U
  American Indian History II, University of Minnesota, U
American Studies
  American Cultures II, University of Minnesota, U
  American Cultures III, University of Minnesota, U
  Ellery Queen & the American Detective Story, University of
    Minnesota, U

Animal Sciences
  Food Analysis, Kansas State University, U, G
  Fundamentals of Food Processing, Kansas State University, U
  Fundamentals of Nutrition, Kansas State University, U
  Horse Production, University of Missouri, U
  Introduction to Food Science, Kansas State University, U
  Principles of Meat Science, Kansas State University, U
Anthropology
  General Anthropology, University of Missouri, U
  Human Origins, University of Minnesota, U
  Human Origins and Evolution, University of Texas, U
  Introduction to Folklore, University of Missouri, U
  Physical Anthropology, University of Texas, U
Architecture
  Romanesque, Gothic and Renaissance Architecture, University of
    Washington, U
Art
  Art Worlds, Governors State University, U
  Drawing & Design Fundamentals, Eastern Oregon State
    College, U
  Foundations of Visual Literacy, Eastern Oregon State
    College, U
  The Gallery Electric, Governors State University, U, G
  Introduction to the Visual Arts, University of Minnesota, U
Astronomy
  Astronomy, University of Washington, U
  Introduction to General Astronomy, University of California
    Extension, U
  The Planets, University of Washington, U
Atmospheric Science
  Weather, University of Washington, U
Behavioral Sciences
  Introduction to Research Methods & Statistics, University of
    Maryland, U
  Risk, University of Maryland, U
Biological Sciences
  The Biology of Cancer, University of California Extension, U
  General Genetics, University of Missouri, U
  Heredity and Human Society, University of Minnesota, U

Human Anatomy, Eastern Oregon State College, U

Human Physiology, Eastern Oregon State College, U

Principles and Techniques of Molecular Cell Biology, University of California Extension, U

Botany/Plant Science

Basic Home Horticulture, University of Missouri, U

Plant Life in California, University of California Extension, U

Plant Propagation, University of Missouri, U

Theory and Concepts of Plant Pathology, University of Missouri, U

Business

Business Analysis Methods, University of Maryland, U

The Business/Government Relationship, University of Maryland, U

Business Law, Eastern Oregon State College, U

Business and Society: Ethics and Stakeholder Management, University of Minnesota, U

Career Counseling, University of California Extension, N

Effective Personnel Administration, University of California Extension, U

How to Open a Beer Bar or Brewpub, The New School, N

How to Open a Restaurant, The New School, N

Individual Income Taxation, Eastern Oregon State College, U

Information Resource Management, University of California Extension, U

Introduction to Business, Eastern Oregon State College, U

Introduction to Business Law, University of Missouri, U

Introduction to Business Organization and Management, University of California, U

Introduction to International Business, University of California Extension, U

Introduction to Retail Merchandising, University of Minnesota, U

Investment Management, University of California Extension, U

Investments, Eastern Oregon State College, U

Japanese Management, Eastern Oregon State College, U

Management Science, Eastern Oregon State College, U

Non-Profit Accounting, Eastern Oregon State College, U

Principles of Finance, Eastern Oregon State College, U

Report Writing, Eastern Oregon State College, U

Chemistry
    General Chemistry 140, University of Washington, U
    General Chemistry 150, University of Washington, U
    Introduction to General Chemistry, University of Washington, U
    Organic/Biochemistry, Eastern Oregon State College, U
Civil Engineering
    Environmental Behavior of Pollutants, University of California Extension, U
    Pollution Prevention and Waste Minimization, University of California Extension, U
    Technologies for Treatment, Disposal, and Remediation of Hazardous Wastes, University of California Extension, U
Classical Studies
    Classical Mythology, University of Missouri, U
Communications
    History and Development of Communications & Journalism, University of Washington, U
    How to Do Research On Line, The New School, U
    The Internet Made Simple, USDA Graduate School, U
    Internet Navigation, Raritan Valley Community College, U
    Interneting for Biologists and Others, University of Minnesota, U
    Introduction to Mass Media, University of Missouri, U
    Introduction to On-Line Communication, USDA Graduate School, U
    Introduction to Visual Telecommunications, USDA Graduate School, U
    Legal Aspects of Communications, University of Washington, U
    The Phenomena of Communicating, University of Washington, U
    Speeding along the Internet, University of Northern Colorado, N
    Using the Internet: A Tool Kit, University of Illinois at Urbana, N
    Writing for Managers, University of Maryland, U
Computer Science
    Advanced PC Topics, The New School, U
    C Language Programming, The New School, U
    C Language Programming, University of California Extension, U
    C Programming: Introduction and Intermediate, University of Washington, N

Welcome to the SCILS distance education course:

Public Relations Management

194:524 (DE)

NOTICE: This course originally was schedule to run next during Fall semester of 1996 (September through December). It has been postponed to Spring semester of 1997 (January through May). Its place on the fall schedule will be taken by a new course: 194:518 (DE) Organizational Publics and Communication Campaigns, taught by Prof. Todd Hunt. It is anticipated that in the future these two course will run in alternate semesters. Information on the content and focus of the new course and how to register for distance education will be posted on the "DE" section of the SCILS web site by the end of June. New abstracts will continue to be added to DataBank for Public Relations Management from time to time while the course is on hiatus. (6/10/96)

If you're dialing in from home on a SLIP or PPP connection, you probably want to use the text-only version.

If you have a high bandwidth connection, you might want to use the graphics-intensive version.

Here's a link to go back to the S.C.I.L.S. homepage, if you want.

These pages created and maintained by Todd Hunt.

SCILS

Computer Networking, University of Maryland, U
Computers and Society, Thomas Edison State College, U
Concepts of Database Management Systems, University of California
  Extension, U
Concepts of Information Systems, University of California
  Extension, U
Cyberspace: Brave New World, The New School, N
Data Communications, University of Maryland, U

Public Relations Management
a S.C.I.L.S. distance education course

The original design for this web site was created by Silvia Muller, a graduate of the MLS program at SCILS. The graphics were designed by Michael Flynn, a graduate of the MCIS program at SCILS. Thanks also to Jon Oliver, SCILS Computing Services Manager, for administration of the web server.

Table of Contents

Part 1 - Overview and Organization

*About Distance Education
*Course Objectives
*Text and Additional Readings
*Bibliography
*Course Schedule
*Assignments and Deadlines
*Census Form/Class Directory
*Access to Information
*Videotape
*Web Sites of Interest

Part 2 - More About the Assignments and the Simulation

*Section I Case Study
*About "Simulation"
*Welcome to Garden Pride
*Sample test questions
*Second Exam of the Course

Part 3 - Sample Policy Statements

*Sample Policy Statement
*Garden Pride Policy on Crisis Management
*Garden Pride Policy on Crisis Communication
*Crisis Communications Plan-Parking and Transportations Servic\ es Department

Databank of Public Relations Information

Take a look at our Experimental Page for some sounds and video clips.

To go back to the SCILS Home page.

Developing a C Application, University of Washington, N
Distributed Systems, University of Maryland, U
Fundamentals of C++ Programming, University of California
    Extension, U
Fundamentals of Data Communications and Networks, University of
    California Extension, U
Introduction to Programming with BASIC, University of California
    Extension, U
Introductory Pascal, University of California Extension, U
Systems Analysis and Design: An Overview, University of California
    Extension, U
Using the Internet, University of California Extension, U
Using the UNIX Operating System, University of California
    Extension, U
Worldwide Web Page Design and Construction, The New School, U
Criminology/Criminal Justice
    Corrections, University of Missouri, U
    Introduction to Criminology and Criminal Justice, University of
        Missouri, U
    Rights of the Offender, University of Missouri, U
Cultural Studies
    Crossing Cultures: World Views in the Humanities, University of
        Maryland, U
    Cyberpunk: Society in the Age of Information, The New School, U
    Discourse and Society I: Reading Culture, University of Minnesota, U
    Discourse and Society II: Meaning and History, University of
        Minnesota, U
    The Passions, The New School, U
    Postmodernism and Its Critics, The New School, U
Economics
    American Labor and Unions, Eastern Oregon State College, U
    Intermediate Microeconomics, University of Washington, U
    International Economics, Thomas Edison State College, U
    Introduction to the American Economy, University of Missouri, U
    Introduction to Economics II, University of Missouri, U
    Introduction to Macroeconomics, University of California Extension, U
    Introduction to Macroeconomics, University of Washington, U
    Introduction to Microeconomics, University of Washington, U

Managerial Economics, Eastern Oregon State College, U
Money and Banking, Eastern Oregon State College, U
Money and Banking, University of Missouri, U
Principles of Macroeconomics, University of Missouri, U
Education
Adaptive Computer Technology, University of Washington, U
Creating Social Studies Curriculum, University of Minnesota, U
Directed Study: Inventing the Future, University of Minnesota, U
Human Development & Learning, Eastern Oregon State College, U
Science Education: Elementary School Programs and Practices,
University of Washington, U
Second Languages and Young Children, University of Minnesota, U
Secondary Education Seminar: Language Arts, Eastern Oregon State
College, U
The Secondary School Curriculum, University of Missouri, U
Technology in the Classroom, Eastern Illinois University, U
Using the Internet for Curriculum Development, University of
Washington, U
English
Approaches to Grammar, Eastern Oregon State College, U
Twentieth Century English Novel, University of Minnesota, U
Entomology
Insects in the Environment, University of Missouri, U
Principles of Beekeeping, University of Minnesota, U
Environmental Studies
Careers in Environmental Management, University of California
Extension, U
Conservation of Natural Resources, University of Minnesota, U
Environmental Auditing and Assessment, University of California
Extension, U
Environmental Issues, University of California Extension, U
Environmental Regulatory Framework, University of California
Extension, U
Global Environmental Change, Thomas Edison State College, U
Hazardous Materials Emergency Management, University of California
Extension, U
Introduction to Environmental Studies, University of Washington, U
Principles of Hazardous Materials Management, University of

California Extension, U
Toxicology & Risk Assessment for Environmental Decision Making, University of California Extension, U
Extension and Adult Education
Extension Organization and Administration, University of Missouri, U
Fundamentals of Extension Teaching of Adults, University of Missouri, U
Program Development and Evaluation, University of Missouri, U
Film
16mm Film Intensive, The New School, U
American Cinema, Thomas Edison State College, U
The Art of Film History, University of California Extension, U
Screenwriting 1, The New School, U
Screenwriting 2, The New School, U
Finance, Personal
Principles of Finance, University of Missouri, U
Foods and Nutrition
Food Trends, Legislation & Regulation, Kansas State University, U
Sensory Analysis of Foods, Kansas State University, U, G
Gender Studies
Sex, Gender, and Beyond, The New School, U
Women, Reproduction, and Experience, The New School, U
Geography
Cartography I, Eastern Oregon State College, U
Cartography II, Eastern Oregon State College, U
Geography of Cities, University of Washington, U
Geography of Missouri, University of Missouri, U
Physical Geography, University of Missouri, U
Regions and Nations of the World I, University of Missouri, U
Regions and Nations of the World II, University of Missouri, U
World Regions, University of Washington, U
Geology
Earth Science, University of Missouri, U
Earthquakes: Their Geology and Human Impact, University of California Extension, U
Introduction to Geological Sciences, University of Washington, U
Physical Geology, University of Missouri, U

Gerontology
  Biological Aspects of Aging, University of Washington, U
  Social and Cultural Aspects of Aging, University of Washington, U
History
  The 1920s: The Emergence of Modern America, The New School, U
  American Constitutional History I, University of Minnesota, U
  American Constitutional History II, University of Minnesota, U
  American History I, University of Minnesota, U
  American History II, University of Minnesota, U
  Britain, 1688 to the Present, University of Missouri, U
  Civil War and Reconstruction, University of Minnesota, U
  English Civilization before 1603, University of Texas, U
  English Civilization since 1603, University of Texas, U
  First World War, University of Iowa, U
  History of American Foreign Relations, 1760–1865, University of
    Minnesota, U
  History of American Foreign Relations, 1945–1995, University of
    Minnesota, U
  History of Missouri, University of Missouri, U
  History of Modern Japan, University of Washington, U
  History of the Old South, University of Missouri, U
  History of the United States since 1940, University of Washington, U
  Introduction to Modern European History 1, University of
    Minnesota, U
  Introduction to Modern European History 2, University of
    Minnesota, U
  Introduction to Modern European History 3, University of
    Minnesota, U
  The Question of Human Nature, University of Washington, U
  Survey of American History since 1865, University of Missouri, U
  Survey of Civilizations in Ancient Asia, University of Minnesota, U
  Survey of the History of the United States, University of
    Washington, U
  Sweden: 1560–1721, University of Minnesota, U
  Texas and Its History, University of Texas, U
  The United States, 1492–1865, University of Texas, U
  The United States since 1865, University of Texas, U
  The United States in the 20th Century, University of Minnesota, U
  Western Civilization in Medieval Times, University of Texas, U

Western Civilization in Modern Times, University of Texas, U
Western Civilization since 1600, University of Missouri, U
Journalism
Communication and Public Opinion, University of Minnesota, U
High School Journalism, University of Misssouri, U
History of American Journalism, University of Missouri, U
Languages
Beginning Latin I, University of Minnesota, U
Beginning Latin II, University of Minnesota, U
Elementary Italian I, University of Washington, U
Elementary Italian II, University of Washington, U
Elementary Italian III, University of Washington, U
Elementary Spanish I, University of Washington, U
Elementary Spanish II, University of Washington, U
Elementary Spanish III, University of Washington, U
First-Year German I, University of Washington, U
First-Year German II, University of Washington, U
First-Year German III, University of Washington, U
Latin Poetry: Vergil's Aeneid, University of Minnesota, U
Latin Prose & Poetry: Caesar and Others, University of Minnesota, U
Selections from Latin Literature, University of Minnesota, U
Linguistics
Introduction to Grammar, University of Washington, U
Introduction to Language, The New School, U
Introduction to Linguistic Thought, University of Washington, U
Literature
American Fiction, University of California Extension, U
American Literature: Contemporary America, University of
    Washington, U
American Literature: From the Beginnings to 1865, University of
    Texas, U
American Literature: From 1865 to the Present, University of Texas, U
American Literature: The Early Modern Period, University of
    Washington, U
American Literature: The Early Nation, University of Washington, U
American Science Fiction, University of Texas, U
The American Short Story, The New School, U
American Voices: The Next Generation, The New School, U
The Bible as Literature, University of Washington, U

English Literature: The Late Renaissance, University of Washington, U
Fantasy, University of Washington, U
The Gothic, The New School, U
Gothic Fiction, University of Missouri, U
Literary Types, University of Missouri, U
Literature of the New Testament, University of Missouri, U
Literature of the Old Testament, University of Missouri, U
Major Authors (Shakespeare), University of Missouri, U
Masterworks of Literature: American, University of Texas, U
Milton, University of Washington, U
The Modern Novel, University of Washington, U
Multicultural Literature, University of California Extension, U
Reading Fiction, University of Washington, U
Reading Literature, University of Washington, U
Science Fiction (Historical Survey), University of Iowa, U
Shakespeare, University of Washington, U
Shakespeare: Selected Plays, University of Texas, U
Shakespeare to 1603, University of Washington, U
Shakespeare after 1603, University of Washington, U
Shakespeare's Comedies, The New School, U
Wuthering Heights and Jane Eyre: The Novels and the Movies, The New School, U

Management
Entrepreneurship & the Smaller Enterprise, University of Minnesota, U
Fundamentals of Management, University of Minnesota, U
Fundamentals of Management, University of Missouri, U
Human Resource Management, University of Missouri, U
Human-Resources Management, University of Maryland, U
Management: Perspectives, Process, Productivity, University of Maryland, U
Management in a Global Context, University of Maryland, U
Managerial Planning and Competitive Strategies, University of Maryland, U
Managing in Organizations, Thomas Edison State College, U
Managing in the Public Sector, University of Maryland, U
Organization Development, University of Maryland, U
Organizational Communication, University of Maryland, U
Organizational Theory, University of Missouri, U
Principles of Management, Thomas Edison State College, U

Problem Solving, University of Maryland, U
Project Management, University of Maryland, U
Quality Management, University of California Extension, U
Strategic Management, University of Maryland, U
Total Quality Management, University of Maryland, U

Marketing

Fundamentals of Marketing, University of Missouri, U
Introduction to Marketing, Thomas Edison State College, U
Principles of Marketing, University of California Extension, U
Principles of Marketing, University of Maryland, U

Mathematics

Advanced Calculus, University of Illinois at Urbana, U
Algebra with Applications, University of Washington, U
Applications of Calculus to Business and Economics, University of Washington, U
Calculus, University of Illinois at Urbana–Champaign, U
Calculus II, University of Illinois at Urbana–Champaign, U
Calculus and Analytical Geometry, University of Illinois at Urbana–Champaign, U
Differential Equations and Orthogonal Functions, University of Illinois at Urbana–Champaign, U
Elementary Linear Algebra, University of Washington, U
For All Practical Purposes I, Eastern Oregon State College, U
For All Practical Purposes II, Eastern Oregon State College, U
Foundations of Elementary Math I, Eastern Oregon State College, U
Foundations of Elementary Math II, Eastern Oregon State College, U
Foundations of Elementary Math III, Eastern Oregon State College, U
Introduction to Differential Equations, University of Washington, U
Introduction to Statistics, University of California Extension, U
Mathematics: A Practical Art, University of Washington, U
Mathematics: Contemporary Topics & Applications, University of Maryland, U
Precalculus, University of Washington, U

Music

20th Century American Music, University of Minnesota, U
The Avant-Garde, University of Minnesota, U
History of Jazz, University of Washington, U
Listening to Music through the Ages, The New School, U

Nursing
  Life Span Growth and Development I, University of Minnesota, U
  Life Span Growth and Development II, University of Minnesota, U
Nutrition
  The New Nutrition, University of California Extension, U
  Nutrition, Eastern Oregon State College, U
  Nutrition, University of California Extension, U
  Nutrition for Today, University of Washington, U
Oceanography
  Survey of Oceanography, University of Washington, U
Office Administration
  Business Communications, Eastern Oregon State College, U
  Computerized Accounting, Eastern Oregon State College, U
  Desktop Publishing Applications, Eastern Oregon State College, U
  Machine Transcription, Eastern Oregon State College, U
  Math for Business, Eastern Oregon State College, U
  Office Procedures I, Eastern Oregon State College, U
  Office Procedures II, Eastern Oregon State College, U
  Professional Development, Eastern Oregon State College, U
  Wordprocessing: Executive, Eastern Oregon State College, U
  Wordprocessing: Legal, Eastern Oregon State College, U
  Wordprocessing: Medical, Eastern Oregon State College, U
  Wordprocessing I, Eastern Oregon State College, U
  Wordprocessing II, Eastern Oregon State College, U
Philosophy
  Contemporary Ethics, Thomas Edison State College, U
  Critical Thinking, Eastern Oregon State College, U
  Ethics and the Professions, University of Missouri, U
  General Introduction to Philosophy, University of Missouri, U
  History of Western Philosophy, University of California Extension, U
  Introduction to Logic, University of Missouri, U
  Introduction to Logic, University of Washington, U
  Introduction to Philosophy, University of Minnesota, U
  Major Philosophers: From Socrates to Sartre, Thomas Edison State
    College, U
  Philosophical Issues and the Law, University of Washington, U
  The Philosophy of History, The New School, U
  Practical Reasoning, University of Washington, U

Physical Education/Health
  The American Health Care System, University of Missouri, U
  Applied Anatomy, Eastern Oregon State College, U
  Community Responses to Alcohol & Other Drug Problems, University
    of California Extension, U
  Elements of Health Education, University of Missouri, U
  Medical Aspects of Disability for Vocational Counseling, University of
    Washington, U, G
  The Modern Plague: HIV and AIDS, University of California
    Extension, U
  Topics in Health Services Management, University of Missouri, U
Political Science
  American Foreign Policy, University of Washington, U
  American Government and Politics, University of Minnesota, U
  American Institutions, University of California Extension, U
  American National Government, Eastern Oregon State College, U
  American Political Parties, University of Minnesota, U
  Comparative Politics, Eastern Oregon State College, U
  Congress, Eastern Oregon State College, U
  Environmental Politics and Policy in the United States, University of
    Washington, U
  International Relations, Eastern Oregon State College, U
  International Relations, University of Missouri, U
  Introduction to American Government, The New School, U
  Introduction to International Relations, University of Washington, U
  Introduction to Political Science, University of Missouri, U
  Introduction to Politics, University of Washington, U
  Introduction to Public Administration, University of Missouri, U
  Judicial Process, University of Minnesota, U
  The Politics of Mass Communication in America, University of
    Washington, U
  The Politics of the Third World, University of Missouri, U
  Public Administration, Eastern Oregon State College, U
  Public Policy, Eastern Oregon State College, U
  State Government, University of Missouri, U
  State and Local Government, Eastern Oregon State College, U
  The United States Congress, University of Minnesota, U
  U.S. Defense Policy Making, University of Missouri, U

Psychology

    Abnormal Psychology, University of California Extension, U
    Abnormal Psychology, University of Washington, U
    Adolescence, University of California Extension, U
    Adolescent Development, University of Missouri, U
    Adolescent Psychology, University of Minnesota, U
    Adolescent Psychology, University of Missouri, U
    Animal Behavior, University of Missouri, U
    Child Development, University of Missouri, U
    Child Psychology, University of Missouri, U
    Cognitive Psychology, University of Missouri, U
    Criticial Thinking, University of California Extension, U
    Developmental Psychology, University of California Extension, U
    Developmental Psychology, University of Washington, U
    Educational Measurement, University of Missouri, U
    Elementary Psychological Statistics, University of Washington, U
    Environmental Psychology, University of Missouri, U
    Foundations of Educational and Psychological Measurement, University of Missouri, U
    Fundamentals of Psychological Research, University of Washington, U
    General Psychology, University of Missouri, U
    Human Learning, University of Missouri, U
    Industrial Psychology, University of Missouri, U
    Infancy, University of Minnesota, U
    Introduction to Child Psychology, University of Minnesota, U
    Introduction to Drugs and Behavior, University of Washington, U
    Introduction to Personality and Individual Differences, University of Washington, U
    Introduction to Psychopathology, The New School, U
    Introduction to Social Development, University of Minnesota, U
    Learning and Instruction, University of Missouri, U
    Motivation, Eastern Oregon State College, U
    Perception, University of Missouri, U
    Personality Development of the Child, University of Washington, U
    Principles of Development: Lifespan, Eastern Oregon State College, U
    Principles of Learning, Eastern Oregon State College, U
    Psychology as a Social Science, University of Washington, U
    Psychology of Communication, University of California Extension, U

Social Psychology, Thomas Edison State College, U
Social Psychology, University of Washington, U
Survey of Cognitive Psychology, University of Washington, U

Religion

Introduction to World Religions: Eastern Traditions, University of Washington, U
Religions of East Asia, University of Minnesota, U
The Religious Quest, Thomas Edison State College, U
Views of the Absolute in World Religions, University of California Extension, U

Russian

Russian Literature: Middle Ages–Dostoevsky, University of Minnesota, U

Science

Environmental Geology, The New School, U
The Nature of Physics, The New School, U

Social Work

Introduction to American Social Welfare and Community Services, University of Minnesota, U
Policy and Service Delivery in Social Welfare, University of Missouri, U
Social Justice and Social Policy, University of Missouri, U
Social Welfare and Social Work, University of Missouri, U

Sociology

American Indian Folklore and Ceremonial, The New School, U
Criminology, University of Missouri, U
Criminology, University of Washington, U
Cultural Property vs. Cultural Resources, The New School, U
Fundamentals of Archaeology, The New School, U
Introduction to Sociology: Principles, University of Iowa, U
Marriage and the Family, Thomas Edison State College, U
Origins of African-American Religious & Social Thought, The New School, U
Principles of Sociology: A Multicultural Perspective, University of California Extension, U
Rural Sociology, University of Missouri, U
The Social Construction of Identity, The New School, U
Social Justice and Oppression, The New School, U
Socialization, University of Washington, U

Sociology and Social Problems, University of Minnesota, U
Survey of Sociology, University of Washington, U
Urban Sociology, University of Missouri, U
Women in Muslim Society, University of Minnesota, U
Special Education
Introduction to Mental Retardation, University of Missouri, U
Introduction to Special Education, University of Missouri, U
Statistics
Basic Statistics, University of Washington, U
Basic Statistics with Applications, University of Washington, U
Elements of Statistical Methods, University of Washington, U
Introduction to Ideas of Statistics, University of Minnesota, U
Theater Arts
On-Line Humor, The New School, U
Playwriting, The New School, U
Writing
Advanced Expository Writing, University of Washington, U
Applied Discourse Theory, Eastern Oregon State College, U
Beginning Fiction Workshop, The New School, U
Beginning Short Story Writing, University of Washington, U
Composition: Exposition, University of Washington, U
Discourse Theory, Eastern Oregon State College, U
Fiction Writing: Memory, Imagination, Desires, The New School, U
Fiction Writing Workshop, The New School, U
From Silence to Poem, The New School, U
Intermediate Expository Writing, University of Washington, U
Intermediate Seminar: Short Story Writing, University of
    Washington, U
Introduction to Expository Writing, Eastern Oregon State College, U
Introduction to Technical Writing, University of Washington, U
Preparatory Writing, The New School, U
Reading for Writing, The New School, U
Screenwriting Fundamentalism, Eastern Oregon State College, U
Selected Topics in Writing, Eastern Oregon State College, U
Technical Writing, University of California Extension, U
Technical Writing for Engineers, University of Minnesota, U
Topics in Writing, University of Texas, U
Writing about Literature, University of Minnesota, U
Writing about Science, University of Minnesota, U

Writing for the Arts, University of Minnesota, U
Writing for Magazines, The New School, U
Writing Fundamentals, University of California Extension, N
Writing in the Humanities, University of Minnesota, U
Writing in the Social Sciences, University of Minnesota, U
Writing a Successful Essay, University of California Extension, U

HOW TO READ THE DESCRIPTIONS

Following is an explanation of each caption used to describe the online college courses included in the directory.

Institution   The complete name and address of the college, institute, or university sponsoring the courses described.

Accreditation   The name of the association that has accredited the institution, as well as the association accrediting individual programs where appropriate. Only schools accredited by an association recognized by the U.S. Department of Education and/or the Council on Recognition of Postsecondary Accreditation are included in this directory.

Hardware Requirements   Any hardware required to take online courses from each school.

Software Requirements   Any software required to take online courses from each school.

Remarks   Specific comments concerning the school or courses that are not covered by the other captions.

Subject Area   Subject areas for each school are identical to those used in the preceding course locator.

Course Title   The title of each online course available from the institution.

Prerequisite   The minimum requirements for enrolling in this course, plus any policies in force for waiving them.

Credit Value   The number of undergraduate or graduate credits you can earn by successfully completing this course.

Tuition   Either the total cost for completing the course or the per-credit tuition charge. These are basic costs that generally do not include books and other fees normally charged by colleges for various services provided to students. Keep in mind that all institutions reserve the right to change their tuition and fees at any time, so consider this as a general guide to what the online course will cost.

Description   A brief but informative description of what the course covers and what students may expect to learn from it.

FULL DESCRIPTIONS OF ONLINE COLLEGE COURSES

EASTERN ILLINOIS UNIVERSITY

Off Campus and Contract Programs
Charleston, IL 61920-3099
Telephone: (217) 581-5114
Fax: (217) 581-6697
Web Site: http://www.eiu.edu/

Accreditation   North Central Association of Colleges and Schools

Hardware Requirements   IBM® or compatible or Macintosh® with communications capability

Software Requirements   Netscape or similar communications software

Remarks   The university participates, along with others in the state, in the Board of Governors Universities External Degree Program.

EDUCATION

Technology in the Classroom, EDF 4998-120

Prerequisite   A basic understanding of, and access to, the Internet and World Wide Web.

Credit Value   3 semester hours of undergraduate credit

Tuition $275

Description   Intended to broaden participants' knowledge of instructional technologies and explore ways of integrating them into the curriculum.

EASTERN OREGON STATE COLLEGE

Division of Extended Programs
1410 "L" Avenue
LaGrande, OR 97850-2899
Telephone: (541) 962-3378
Fax: (541) 962-3627
Web Site: http://www.eosc.osshe.edu/
E-mail: jhart@eosc.asshe.edu

Accreditation   Northwest Association of Schools and Colleges

Hardware Requirements   IBM or IBM-compatible with Windows 3.1 or later, or a Macintosh Plus or later computer with System 6.0.3 or later, and a modem

EASTERN ILLINOIS UNIVERSITY

Welcome to the EIU President's Page	News, Publications, and Calendars	Campus Information
Communicating with EIU People	Administrative and Departmental Information	Colleges
Student Services, Activities, and Regulations	Library Services	Information Technology Services
Interested in Attending Eastern?	Community Kiosk	What's Cool at EIU
Eastern Alumni	What's New at EIU?	

Last updated August 28, 1996

webmaster

Column, books, and glasses © PhotoDisc, Inc. 1996

Software Requirements   Word-processing software capable of saving files in a pure text (ASCII) format

Remarks   The college offers several external degree programs leading to bachelor's degrees. Where appropriate, the credits earned in these courses may be applied toward one of these degrees. Courses offered by Eastern Oregon are based on computer conferencing.

ART

Drawing & Design Fundamentals, ART 129
Prerequisite   None
Credit Value   5 undergraduate quarter credits
Tuition $435

Description   Introduces basic drawing techniques, gesture, perspective, rendering, and the interaction of the elements of design.

Foundations of Visual Literacy, ART 101
Prerequisite   None
Credit Value   5 undergraduate quarter credits
Tuition $415
Description   Designed to increase visual literacy, this course familiarizes participants with terms and techniques associated with the usage of visual media.

BIOLOGICAL SCIENCES

Human Anatomy, BIOL 231
Prerequisite   Previous chemistry courses
Credit Value   4 undergraduate quarter credits
Tuition $370
Description   An examination of the gross and microscopic anatomy of the human body. Includes the nervous, skeletal, circulatory, gastrointestinal, renal, reproductive, and integumentary systems.

Human Physiology, BIOL 232
Prerequisite   Previous chemistry courses
Credit Value   4 undergraduate quarter credits
Tuition $370
Description   An introduction to the principles of human physiology, including homeostatic control mechanisms and their functions, and the fundamental interrelationships between interacting systems. Includes an introduction to cell biology.

BUSINESS

Business Law, BA 254
Prerequisite   None
Credit Value   4 undergraduate quarter credits
Tuition $325
Description   Studies the nature, origin, and philosophy of law and procedures. Also studies law of contracts and sales.

Individual Income Taxation, BA 333
Prerequisite   Managerial Accounting course
Credit Value   5 undergraduate quarter credits
Tuition $405
Description   Studies the federal income tax system, including its historical development, tax research techniques, and tax planning.

Introduction to Business, BA 101
Prerequisite None
Credit Value 5 undergraduate quarter credits
Tuition $405
Description An introduction to the role of business in society, its historical roots, and the major functional areas of business.

Japanese Management, BA 407
Prerequisite None
Credit Value 5 undergraduate quarter credits
Tuition $405
Description A cultural and managerial study of Japanese management techniques and their applicability to the U.S. economy.

Management Science, BA 366
Prerequisite Math and statistics courses
Credit Value 5 undergraduate quarter credits
Tuition $460
Description Studies the management decision-making process using mathematical models and computer software. Includes Linear Programming, PERT/CPM, Inventory Management, Queuing, Decision Theory, Forecasting, and others.

Non-Profit Accounting, BA 420
Prerequisite None
Credit Value 3 undergraduate quarter credits
Tuition $425
Description In-depth examination of the principles, theory, and procedures applicable to accounting for nonprofit organizations.

Principles of Finance, BA 313
Prerequisite None
Credit Value 5 undergraduate quarter credits
Tuition $415
Description An introduction that focuses on the allocation of resources for investment in short- and long-term assets, decisions with respect to debt and equity financing, and dividend policy and securities decisions.

Report Writing, BA 225
Prerequisite None
Credit Value 4 undergraduate quarter credits
Tuition $325
Description Analyzes the methods of investigating, collecting, organizing, and presenting data for formal and informal business reports.

CHEMISTRY

Organic/Biochemistry, CHEM 211
Prerequisite   An introductory chemistry course
Credit Value   3 undergraduate quarter credits
Tuition $280
Description   A survey of organic chemistry and biochemistry as applied to biology, agriculture, and nursing. Organic compounds of medical importance, macromolecules, metabolic pathways, vitamins, and hormones are studied.

ECONOMICS

American Labor and Unions, ECON 481
Prerequisite   None
Credit Value   5 undergraduate quarter credits
Tuition $405
Description   Focuses on the history and development of labor and labor unions in the United States. Examines the theoretical aspects of the labor market and the legislation that governs the labor/management relationship.

Managerial Economics, ECON 340
Prerequisite   Economics, math, and statistics courses
Credit Value   5 undergraduate quarter credits
Tuition $455
Description   Examines an economic approach to decisions involving production, cost, resource allocation, pricing, and long-range forecasting in public and private organizations.

Money and Banking, ECON 318
Prerequisite   A course in principles of macroeconomics
Credit Value   5 undergraduate quarter credits
Tuition $450
Description   Investigates the operation of financial institutions and government agencies that regulate them as they affect the stability of the money supply, financing of government operations, and the impact of taxation.

EDUCATION

Human Development & Learning, ED 316
Prerequisite   Instructor's consent
Credit Value   3 undergraduate quarter credits
Tuition $275
Description   Discusses principles of human development, how learners acquire understanding, and how teachers may enhance the process. There are two versions of this course, one for Education majors and one for all others.

Secondary Education Seminar: Language Arts, ED 463
Prerequisite   None
Credit Value   2 undergraduate quarter credits
Tuition $165
Description   A seminar designed to acquaint students with the curriculum, materials, and supportive resources used in secondary language arts classes.

ENGLISH

Approaches to Grammar, ENG 316
Prerequisite   None
Credit Value   4 undergraduate quarter credits
Tuition $325
Description   Studies traditional and nontraditional approaches to grammar with specific applications to and illustrations from the field of composition.

GEOGRAPHY

Cartography I, GEOG 201
Prerequisite   Two introductory geography classes
Credit Value   3 undergraduate quarter credits
Tuition $260
Description   An entry-level survey of the physical properties and uses of topographic maps and air photographs.

Cartography II, GEOG 306
Prerequisite   Cartography I, GEOG 201
Credit Value   5 undergraduate quarter credits
Tuition $420
Description   A introduction to thematic map construction, including map design, compilation of data, and lettering techniques.

MATHEMATICS

For All Practical Purposes I, MATH 110
Prerequisite   A course in algebraic foundations or its equivalent
Credit Value   4 undergraduate quarter credits
Tuition $375
Description   Designed to bring some of the methods and applications of modern mathematics to the nonspecialist.

For All Practical Purposes II, MATH 110
Prerequisite   For All Practical Purposes I course

Credit Value   4 undergraduate quarter credits
Tuition $375
Description   A continuation of above listed course. Includes election theory, weighted voting, games of conflict, and conic sections and measurements.

Foundations of Elementary Math I, MATH 211
Prerequisite   A course in algebraic foundations or its equivalent
Credit Value   4 undergraduate quarter credits
Tuition $370
Description   An introduction to the basic concepts of elementary mathematics designed to initiate the building of an understanding and appreciation of the nature, structure, philosophy, and history of mathematics.

Foundations of Elementary Math II, MATH 212
Prerequisite   Foundations of Elementary Math I, MATH 211
Credit Value   4 undergraduate quarter credits
Tuition $370
Description   A continuation of MATH 211.

Foundations of Elementary Math III, MATH 213
Prerequisite   Foundations of Elementary Math II, MATH 212
Credit Value   4 undergraduate quarter credits
Tuition $360
Description   A continuation of MATH 212.

NUTRITION

Nutrition, PEH 325
Prerequisite   None
Credit Value   4 undergraduate quarter credits
Tuition $338
Description   Discusses the essential dietary needs of individuals at different ages. Includes dietary analysis and diet planning.

OFFICE ADMINISTRATION

Business Communications, OADM 225
Prerequisite   None
Credit Value   3 undergraduate quarter credits
Tuition $245
Description   Covers written communications in the business environment, including correspondence in sales, collections, bad news, and promotion letters and memos.

Computerized Accounting, OADM 210
Prerequisite   None
Credit Value   3 undergraduate quarter credits
Tuition $ 245
Description   Discusses the principles of accounting applied to a computerized environment using accounting software and the personal computer.

Desktop Publishing, OADM 210
Prerequisite   None
Credit Value   3 undergraduate quarter credits
Tuition $245
Description   Develops basic desktop publishing skills using basic and intermediate PageMaker® features to create a variety of projects.

Machine Transcription, OADM 222
Prerequisite   A basic touch-typing course
Credit Value   5 undergraduate quarter credits
Tuition $410
Description   Develops skills required in the use of machine transcription equipment, including grammar, punctuation, and proofreading.

Math for Business, OADM 210
Prerequisite   None
Credit Value   3 undergraduate quarter credits
Tuition $245
Description   An introduction to business math using electronic printing calculators and microcomputers.

Office Procedures I, OADM 261
Prerequisite   None
Credit Value   5 undergraduate quarter credits
Tuition $405
Description   Studies and applies the principles, procedures, and tools necessary to establish and use administrative and office services.

Office Procedures II, OADM 262
Prerequisite   Office Procedures I, OADM 261
Credit Value   5 undergraduate quarter credits
Tuition $405
Description   A continuation of OADM 261, with emphasis on travel and conference responsibilities, organizing business data, and financial and legal reports.

Professional Development, OADM 264
Prerequisite   Office Procedures II, OADM 262

Credit Value   3 undergraduate quarter credits

Tuition $245

Description   Designed to help students recognize the importance of intellectual, social, and emotional dimensions in business situations. Emphasis is placed on oral and nonverbal communications, ethics, and personal development.

Wordprocessing: Executive, OADM 210

Prerequisite   Word Processing II, OADM 123, and Machine Transcription, OADM 222

Credit Value   5 undergraduate quarter credits

Tuition $429

Description   Designed to familiarize students with the duties performed by executive and administrative secretaries.

Wordprocessing: Legal, OADM 210

Prerequisite   Word Processing II, OADM 123, and Machine Transcription, OADM 222

Credit Value   5 undergraduate quarter credits

Tuition $468

Description   Intended to provide a knowledge of, and understanding of, approximately 800 terms commonly used in the legal profession and how to use them in proper context.

Wordprocessing: Medical, OADM 210

Prerequisite   Word Processing II, OADM 123, and Machine Transcription, OADM 222

Credit Value   5 undergraduate quarter credits

Tuition $459

Description   Designed to provide a clear understanding of the meaning and use of the language of medicine to prepare for employment in a medical office.

Word Processing I, OADM 123

Prerequisite   A basic typing course

Credit Value   2 undergraduate quarter credits

Tuition $165

Description   An introduction to word-processing software using Word-Perfect.

Word Processing II, OADM 124

Prerequisite   Word Processing I, OADM 123

Credit Value   2 undergraduate quarter credits

Tuition $165

Description Teaches advanced word-processing techniques, including merging, math functions, and desktop publishing.

PHILOSOPHY

Critical Thinking, PHIL 203
Prerequisite None
Credit Value 5 undergraduate quarter credits
Tuition $460
Description An introduction to critical thinking and argument analysis, with the primary goal of developing a technique for the evaluation of practical arguments in the real world.

PHYSICAL EDUCATION/HEALTH

Applied Anatomy, PEH 231
Prerequisite Human Anatomy, BIOL 231, or Human Physiology, BIOL 232
Credit Value 3 undergraduate quarter credits
Tuition $250
Description A study of the musculoskeletal structure of the living human body: bones and their articulation and muscles and their actions.

POLITICAL SCIENCE

American National Government, POLS 101
Prerequisite None
Credit Value 5 undergraduate quarter credits
Tuition $405
Description An introductory analysis of U.S. politics, including its historical and philosophical origins and contemporary issues.

Comparative Politics, POLS 200
Prerequisite None
Credit Value 5 undergraduate quarter credits
Tuition $405
Description An introduction to the comparative study of different political cultures and institutions around the world.

Congress, POLS 311
Prerequisite None
Credit Value 3 undergraduate quarter credits
Tuition $245
Description A study of the decision-making processes in legislative bodies, with an emphasis on the U.S. Congress.

International Relations, POLS 221
Prerequisite None
Credit Value 5 undergraduate quarter credits
Tuition $405
Description Examines the contemporary nation–state system with an emphasis on the sources of national power, the causes of war, and the prospects for peace.

Public Administration, POLS 351
Prerequisite None
Credit Value 5 undergraduate quarter credits
Tuition $405
Description An investigation of the role of public management in the political process.

Public Policy, POLS 350
Prerequisite None
Credit Value 5 undergraduate quarter credits
Tuition $405
Description An evaluation of the U.S. political system, this course follows individual programs from their origins and design through implementation.

State and Local Government, POLS 314
Prerequisite None
Credit Value 5 undergraduate quarter credits
Tuition $425
Description An analysis of the politics and organization of U.S. state and local governments.

PSYCHOLOGY

Motivation, PSY 345
Prerequisite A course in general psychology
Credit Value 5 undergraduate quarter credits
Tuition $405
Description An upper division survey of motivational concepts and behavior across areas of psychology. Not a course in self-motivation.

Principles of Development: Lifespan, PSY 311
Prerequisite None
Credit Value 5 undergraduate quarter credits
Tuition $440
Description Discusses the principles of human development from birth to old age, including physical, intellectual, and social development.

Principles of Learning, PSY 343
Prerequisite   A course in general psychology
Credit Value   5 undergraduate quarter credits
Tuition $410
Description   A survey of modern learning and conditioning principles.

WRITING

Applied Discourse Theory, WR 206
Prerequisite   An introductory course in literature and/or writing
Credit Value   3 undergraduate quarter credits
Tuition $245
Description   A study of the theoretical approaches and materials for composition studies. Emphasis on analyzing texts and applying discourse theory to students' own writing.

Introduction to Expository Writing, WR 115
Prerequisite   An essay
Credit Value   4 undergraduate quarter credits
Tuition $325
Description   Provides intensive college-level practice in writing for students with precollege skills.

Screenwriting Fundamentals, WR 310
Prerequisite   None
Credit Value   4 undergraduate quarter credits
Tuition $330
Description   Introduces the process of conceiving, pitching, developing, and writing screenplays appropriate for marketing in the contemporary Hollywood film environment.

Selected Topics in Writing, WR 210
Prerequisite   None
Credit Value   2 undergraduate quarter credits
Tuition $165
Description   Prepares students for writing and writing-intensive courses beyond freshman composition and for taking the Writing Proficiency Examination.

GOVERNORS STATE UNIVERSITY

Media-Based Instruction
University Parkway

University Park, IL 60466-0975
Telephone: (708) 534-5000
Fax: (708) 534-8458
Web Site: http://www.bgu.edu/

Accreditation North Central Association of Colleges and Schools
Hardware Requirements Any personal computer with communications capability
Software Requirements Any communications software
Remarks The university is part of the Board of Governors State Universities system, which includes four other state universities. Governors State is an upper division university, so all students must be at the junior or senior level or be graduate students.

ART

Art Worlds, ART 450
Prerequisite None
Credit Value 3 undergraduate semester hour credits
Tuition $276
Description Compares art objects from seven different contexts and diverse areas of the world. For further information, the course-direct e-mail address is a-bourge@acs.gsu.bgu.edu.

The Gallery Electric, S ART 50F
Prerequisite See Description
Credit Value 3 undergraduate semester hour credits or 3 graduate credits
Tuition Varies
Description Offered through the Division of Fine and Performing Arts, this is an art discussion and criticism course. Participants must be able to visit Chicago exhibition sites to view the work being discussed.

KANSAS STATE UNIVERSITY

Distance Learning Office
231 College Court Building
Manhattan, KS 66506-6007
Telephone: (913) 532-5686 or (800) 622-2KSU
Fax: (913) 532-5637
Web Site: http://www.dce.ksu.edu/
E-mail: distance@dce.ksu.edu

Accreditation North Central Association of Colleges and Schools
Hardware Requirements Any IBM-compatible or Macintosh personal computer with communications capability

Software Requirements Communications software provided by the university

Remarks The university offers an external bachelor's degree completion program for those individuals who have already earned at least 60 undergraduate credits. The following courses can be used toward earning a degree.

ANIMAL SCIENCES

Food Analysis, ASI 725
Prerequisite An introductory food chemistry course
Credit Value 3 undergraduate or 3 graduate credits
Tuition $318 for undergraduates, $432 for graduates
Description Teaches the principles, methods, and techniques necessary for quantitative, physical, and chemical analyses of food and food products relating to food-processing regulations.

Fundamentals of Food Processing, ASI 305
Prerequisite A basic chemistry course
Credit Value 3 undergraduate credits
Tuition $318
Description Studies basic concepts of industrial food processing and preservation, with emphasis on basic ingredients used in food processing and preserving.

Fundamentals of Nutrition, ASI 318
Prerequisite A basic chemistry or biochemistry course
Credit Value 3 undergraduate credits
Tuition $318
Description Teaches the elementary principles of comparative nutrition of farm animals.

Introduction to Food Science, ASI 302
Prerequisite None
Credit Value 3 undergraduate credits
Tuition $318
Description Beginning course in food science designed to acquaint students with the breadth and scope of the food industry and the role of science in the industry.

Principles of Meat Science, ASI 340
Prerequisite A basic chemistry course
Credit Value 2 undergraduate credits

Tuition $214
Description An introduction to the red meat industry in which the fundamental properties of muscle structure, chemistry, and physiology are related to meat quality, composition, and processing.

FOODS & NUTRITION

Food Trends, Legislation and Regulation, FN 301
Prerequisite None
Credit Value 3 undergraduate credits
Tuition $318
Description Studies basic food laws, both historic and current, and the agencies that regulate them. Included are regulations concerning labeling, food additives, and residues.

Sensory Analysis of Foods, FN 701
Prerequisite A basic food nutrition course
Credit Value 3 undergraduate or 3 graduate credits
Tuition $318 for undergraduates, $432 for graduates
Description Provides an awareness of differences in analytical and consumer product testing for obtaining data from human subjects.

THE NEW SCHOOL FOR SOCIAL RESEARCH

Distance Learning Program (DIAL)
68 Fifth Avenue
New York, NY 10011
Telephone: (212) 229-5880 or (800) 319-4321, ext. A30
Fax: (212) 229-5648
Web Site: http://dialnsa.edu/home.html
E-mail: info@dialnsa.edu

Accreditation Middle States Association of Colleges and Schools
Hardware Requirements Any personal computer with communications capability
Software Requirements Any communications software with an Internet connection
Remarks The New School was founded in 1919 as a center for "discussion, instruction, and counseling for mature men and women." Approximately 40,000 adult students attend the school annually or participate in its extensive distance learning programs.

BUSINESS

How to Open a Beer Bar or Brewpub, CULN 0802
Prerequisite None
Credit Value Noncredit
Tuition $109
Description Provides a step-by-step plan for opening a successful beer-based bar or restaurant. Topics include financial requirements, business plans, licenses and permits, equipment, and brewing processes.

How to Open a Restaurant, CULN 0609
Prerequisite None
Credit Value Noncredit
Tuition $211
Description Designed to assist aspiring restauranteurs, this course covers concept development, site selection, staffing, financial requirements, and preparation of a business plan.

COMMUNICATIONS

How to Do Research On Line, FILM 0172
Prerequisite None
Credit Value 3 undergraduate credits
Tuition $330
Description Identifies what is available online, how to find what you need, and how to quickly assess what you have located for quality and reliability.

COMPUTER SCIENCE

Advanced PC Topics, DATA 5571
Prerequisite PC and MS-DOS: An introductory course or similar experience
Credit Value 3 undergraduate credits
Tuition $520
Description Examines new developments and important issues in the computer industry, including technological and marketing trends.

C Language Programming, DATA 0004
Prerequisite Familiarity with at least one other programming language
Credit Value 3 undergraduate credits
Tuition $520
Description Using Borland C, this course covers its language construct, data structures, and operators.

Cyberspace: Brave New World, DATA 5569
Prerequisite None

Credit Value Noncredit
Tuition $290
Description Provides a forum for the discussion of some of the more important issues created by high technology.

Worldwide Web Page Design and Construction, DATA 5584
Prerequisite Basic personal computer experience
Credit Value Noncredit
Tuition $290
Description Introduces HTML (Hypertext language) on the Internet and demonstrates techniques and tips for creating high-impact home pages on the World Wide Web.

CULTURAL STUDIES

Cyberpunk: Society in the Age of Information, SOC 0571
Prerequisite None
Credit Value 3 undergraduate credits
Tuition $330
Description Examines Cyberpunk (technologically driven science fiction) in fiction, film, video, and computer media, including commercially available software.

The Passions, SOC 0508
Prerequisite None
Credit Value 3 undergraduate credits
Tuition $330
Description A study of the "passions of the soul" through readings of Aristotle, Descartes, Spinoza, Heiddegger, and others.

Postmodernism and Its Critics, SOC 0306
Prerequisite None
Credit Value 3 undergraduate credits
Tuition $330
Description An examination of the debates of postmodernism, including various social critics and philosophers, such as Giddens, Habermas, and Harvey.

FILM

16mm Film Intensive, FILM 3351
Prerequisite None
Credit Value 6 undergraduate credits
Tuition $1,315

Description   An intensive workshop introducing all aspects of filmmaking, including production and editing.

Screenwriting I, FILM 0356
Prerequisite   None
Credit Value   3 undergraduate credits
Tuition $415
Description   An introduction to dramatic writing for feature films and television. Also includes a discussion on how to get an agent and the current requirements of the marketplace.

Screenwriting II, FILM 0357
Prerequisite   Screenwriting I or equivalent
Credit Value   3 undergraduate credits
Tuition $415
Description   Focuses on methodology: enhancing original characterization, plot development, conflict, story pacing, and dramatic foreshadowing.

GENDER STUDIES

Sex, Gender, and Beyond, SOCS 0576
Prerequisite   None
Credit Value   3 undergraduate credits
Tuition $330
Description   Examines questions of gender inequality in contemporary life, with particular attention to the way people's personal experiences are both influenced by invisible social forces and reshaped through human action.

Women, Reproduction, and Experience, SOCS 0577
Prerequisite   None
Credit Value   3 undergraduate credits
Tuition $330
Description   Explores the range of women's reproductive experience—conception, contraception, pregnancy, infertility, birth, lactation, and parenting.

HISTORY

The 1920s: The Emergence of Modern America, SOCS 0023
Prerequisite   None
Credit Value   3 undergraduate credits
Tuition $330
Description   Explores a period shaped by issues that continue to this day, including race, nativism, organized crime, and religious fundamentalism.

LINGUISTICS

Introduction to Language, ENLI 0300
Prerequisite None
Credit Value 3 undergraduate credits
Tuition $330
Description Introduces the nature and structure of human language, its biological and social aspects, and the new approaches to syntax and meaning.

LITERATURE

The American Short Story, HUMN 0180
Prerequisite None
Credit Value 3 undergraduate credits
Tuition $330
Description Examines modern masters of the short story, including Anderson, Hemingway, Fitzgerald, Porter, Faulkner, Updike, and Malamud.

American Voices: The Next Generation, HUMN 0564
Prerequisite None
Credit Value 3 undergraduate credits
Tuition $330
Description Examines the work of writers who are setting new standards for American poetry and prose, including Nicholson Baker, Sandra Cisneros, Li-Young Lee, and Erin Belieu.

The Gothic, HUMN 0188
Prerequisite None
Credit Value 3 undergraduate credits
Tuition $330
Description An examination of a variety of gothic fictions, including the work of Walpole, Lewis, Shelley, Poe, and Alcott.

Shakespeare's Comedies: Love, Cross-Dressing, Transformation, HUMN 0102
Prerequisite None
Credit Value 3 undergraduate credits
Tuition $330
Description Explores the darker side of Shakespeare's work in *Two Gentlemen from Verona, The Merchant of Venice, Cymbeline,* and others.

Wuthering Heights and Jane Eyre: The Novels & the Movies, HUMN 0563
Prerequisite None
Credit Value 3 undergraduate credits
Tuition $330

Description A study of the impact of these two novels, including reading them and viewing as many film versions as possible.

MUSIC

Listening to Music through the Ages, MUSA 0102
Prerequisite None
Credit Value 3 undergraduate credits
Tuition $330
Description A survey of Western music from medieval through Baroque, classical, and romantic to contemporary.

PHILOSOPHY

The Philosophy of History, HUMN 0570
Prerequisite None
Credit Value 3 undergraduate credits
Tuition $330
Description Examines the challenges faced by historians in attempting to recreate the past drawing on works by Collingwood, Hegel, and Berlin, among others.

POLITICAL SCIENCE

Introduction to American Government, SOCS 0092
Prerequisite None
Credit Value 3 undergraduate credits
Tuition $330
Description A comprehensive introduction to U.S. national political institutions, debates, and processes. Includes an analysis of the Constitution and the policy-making institutions of the three formal branches of government.

PSYCHOLOGY

Introduction to Psychopathology, SOCS 0574
Prerequisite None
Credit Value 3 undergraduate credits
Tuition $330
Description An introduction to the five basic groupings of psychopathology and to the various therapeutic modalities associated with each.

SCIENCE

Environmental Geology, MASC 0045
Prerequisite None
Credit Value 3 undergraduate credits

Tuition $330

Description Emphasizes the interrelationship of humans with their planet. This course is designed to provide the nonscientist with an understanding of how natural geological processes influence human activity.

The Nature of Physics, MASC 0028
Prerequisite None
Credit Value 3 undergraduate credits
Tuition $330
Description Designed for people who feel physics is too complicated to learn, this course uses simple and easy-to-understand terms to teach students how to analyze factors such as motion, torque, and momentum.

SOCIOLOGY

American Indian Folklore and Ceremonial, SOCS 0225
Prerequisite None
Credit Value 3 undergraduate credits
Tuition $330
Description Explores the poetic range and depth of traditional Native American verbal art, including songs, tales, myths, and legends.

Cultural Property vs Cultural Resources, SOCS 0491
Prerequisite None
Credit Value 3 undergraduate credits
Tuition $330
Description Focuses on the debates concerning who has ownership rights to items collected for museums, how archaeological sites can be protected from looters, the rights of collectors, and the development of legislation affecting these questions.

Fundamentals of Archaeology, SOCS 0196
Prerequisite None
Credit Value 3 undergraduate credits
Tuition $330
Description Topics include how archaeologists find sites, how a typical excavation project functions, what happens to the artifacts uncovered, and the rights of indigenous people.

Origins of African-American Religious & Social Thought, SOCS 0532
Prerequisite None
Credit Value 3 undergraduate credits
Tuition $330
Description Examines the Black experience during the American Revolu-

tion, slavery, early abolition of slavery in certain states, the creation of religious and social institutions in the Black community, and how these have influenced religious and social thought.

The Social Construction of Identity, SOCS 0472
Prerequisite   None
Credit Value   3 undergraduate credits
Tuition $330
Description   Addresses the development of identity for women, and considers the influence of social discourse in the development of self.

Social Justice and Oppression, SOCS 0120
Prerequisite   None
Credit Value   3 undergraduate credits
Tuition $330
Description   The study of oppression and social justice through literature, including works by John Rawls, D. H. Lawrence, William Golding, and Alan Paton.

THEATER ARTS

On-Line Humor, THTR 0452
Prerequisite   None
Credit Value   1 undergraduate credit
Tuition $165
Description   A workshop exploring humorous ways for students to apply their talents and training in a variety of applications on the Internet, including locating sources of specific humor and inserting personal humor into online communications.

Playwriting, THTR 0444
Prerequisite   None
Credit Value   3 undergraduate credits
Tuition $340
Description   An introduction to basic drama, including story, character, conflict, scene construction, and overall plotting. Students should expect to complete at least twenty pages of script by the end of the course.

WRITING

Beginning Fiction Workshop, WRIT 0132
Prerequisite   None
Credit Value   3 undergraduate credits

Tuition $385

Description   Designed to help the beginner through assignments to inspire writing and elements of craft such as character, dialogue, scene, and narrative point of view.

Fiction Writing Workshop, WRIT 0133
Prerequisite   None
Credit Value   3 undergraduate credits
Tuition $385
Description   Most of the time in this course is spent in practice writing and criticizing the works of other students. The goal is to end the course with at least one or two stories or chapters completed.

From Silence to Poem, WRIT 0175
Prerequisite   None
Credit Value   3 undergraduate credits
Tuition $385
Description   Designed to help students, both beginning and advanced writers, to dismantle silences in their lives and generate poems from their personal experiences.

Preparatory Writing, WRIT 0335
Prerequisite   None
Credit Value   3 undergraduate credits
Tuition $385
Description   A workshop for the new, rusty, or uncertain writer, focuses on nonfiction. Students review fundamentals such as grammar, punctuation, and usage, while working on their own pieces.

Reading for Writing, WRIT 0009
Prerequisite   None
Credit Value   3 undergraduate credits
Tuition $385
Description   Examines several short pieces of literature selected from a wide range of genres. Students are then assigned to write their own pieces in a style similar to that of each examined piece.

Writing for Magazines, FILM 0351
Prerequisite   None
Credit Value   3 undergraduate credits
Tuition $360
Description   A workshop for people who have writing skills and want to break into magazine journalism. Includes how to develop an idea into a publishable article and how to pitch a story.

RARITAN VALLEY COMMUNITY COLLEGE

Business Administration/C.I.S. Departments
P.O. Box 3300
Somerville, NJ 08876-1265
Telephone: (908) 526-1200, ext. 8288
Fax: (908) 231-8811
Web Site: http://raritanval.edu/

Accreditation   Middle States Association of Colleges and Schools
Hardware Requirements   Any personal computer with a modem
Software Requirements   Most popular communications software will work
Remarks   This community college, located in western New Jersey, offers personal computer owners a unique opportunity to learn how to use the Internet for fun and work.

COMMUNICATIONS

Internet Navigation
Prerequisite   None
Credit Value   3 undergraduate credits
Tuition $390 for New Jersey residents, $750 for nonresidents
Description   Provides instruction for using the Internet to send both local and global e-mail, to navigate the Internet to do research, and to use the Internet just for fun.

SOUTHERN ILLINOIS UNIVERSITY AT CARBONDALE

Division of Continuing Education
Mailcode 6705
Carbondale, IL 62901-6705
Telephone: (618) 536-7751 or (800) 818-2732
Fax: (618) 453-5680

Accreditation   North Central Association of Colleges and Schools
Requirements   Available only on GOPHER but will soon be on the World Wide Web
Remarks   In addition to the following course, this state university has a number of correspondence-based undergraduate courses.

AGRICULTURE

Introduction to Computers in Agriculture, AGEM 318
Prerequisite   None

Credit Value   3 undergraduate credits
Tuition $195
Description   An introductory course on the use of computers in agriculture, focusing on a basic understanding of microcomputers and how to use them to save time and money and increase efficiency.

THOMAS EDISON STATE COLLEGE

Center for Distance & Independent Adult Learning
101 West State Street
Trenton, NJ 08608-1176
Telephone: (609) 292-6317
Fax: (609) 777-0477
Web Site: http://www.tesc.edu/
E-mail: into@call.tesc.edu

Accreditation   Middle States Association of Colleges and Schools
Hardware Requirements   Any personal computer with a modem
Software Requirements   The college provides its own software to enrolled online students that automates direct, toll-free dial-in access
Remarks   All online nonmatriculating students are required to pay a $32 technology fee. Thomas Edison is a nontraditional institution operated by the state of New Jersey. It awards undergraduate and graduate degrees through external programs.

COMPUTER SCIENCE

Computers and Society, OLCOS 161
Prerequisite   Familiarity with at least one software package
Credit Value   6 undergraduate credits
Tuition $336 for New Jersey residents, $492 for nonresidents
Description   Introduces a working vocabulary associated with computers. Course is designed to equip the student with knowledge and skills to be an informed consumer of computing services.

ECONOMICS

International Economics, OLECO 490
Prerequisite   A course in macroeconomics
Credit Value   3 undergraduate credits
Tuition $174 for New Jersey residents, $252 for nonresidents
Description   An in-depth examination of the basic principles of international economics, including industrial policy, strategic trade policy, exchange rate forecasting, and other topics.

ENVIRONMENTAL STUDIES

Global Environmental Change, OLENS 311
Prerequisite   None
Credit Value   6 undergraduate credits
Tuition $336 for New Jersey residents, $492 for nonresidents
Description   Examines a number of environmental changes that may result from human activities and possible effects of and responses to those changes.

FILM

American Cinema, OLFIL 110
Prerequisite   None
Credit Value   3 undergraduate credits
Tuition $174 for New Jersey residents, $252 for nonresidents
Description   An introductory course in film studies through which students learn to become more active and critical viewers. Attempts to help students increase their understanding of films as art and cultural artifacts.

MANAGEMENT

Managing in Organizations, OLMAN 351
Prerequisite   30 semester credits of college-level work
Credit Value   9 undergraduate credits
Tuition $498 for New Jersey residents, $732 for nonresidents
Description   Introduces management in complex organizations, addressing the subject from the systems, behavioral, and management viewpoints.

Principles of Management, OLMAN 301
Prerequisite   None
Credit Value   3 undergraduate credits
Tuition $174 for New Jersey residents, $252 for nonresidents
Description   An introductory course in the concepts of management for those exploring a career in business, government, or educational management. It is intended to provide essential skills in planning and organizing, staffing and directing, controlling, and decision-making.

MARKETING

Introduction to Marketing, OLMAR 301
Prerequisite   None
Credit Value   3 undergraduate credits

Tuition $174 for New Jersey residents, $252 for nonresidents
Description   An introduction to marketing as it relates to contemporary living and society's changing needs. Examines how a marketing manager interacts with diverse areas of business, as well as basic marketing principles.

PHILOSOPHY

Contemporary Ethics, OLPHI 286
Prerequisite   None
Credit Value   3 undergraduate credits
Tuition $174 for New Jersey residents, $252 for nonresidents
Description   Examines contemporary ethical conflicts and provides a grounding in the language, concepts, and traditions of ethics.

Major Philosophers: From Socrates to Sartre, OLPHI 376
Prerequisite   An introduction to philosophy course
Credit Value   3 undergraduate credits
Tuition $174 for New Jersey residents, $252 for nonresidents
Description   Examines six major Western philosophers—Plato, Descartes, Hume, Hegel, Marx, and Sartre—and the way in which each treated real problems of his own time and how they influenced later thinkers dealing with similar problems.

PSYCHOLOGY

Social Psychology, OLPSY 370
Prerequisite   An introduction to psychology course
Credit Value   6 undergraduate credits
Tuition $336 for New Jersey residents, $492 for nonresidents
Description   Surveys the field of social psychology and explores such major topics as communication, friendship, prejudice, conformity, leadership, and aggression.

RELIGION

The Religious Quest, OLREL 405
Prerequisite   30 semester hours of college-level work
Credit Value   9 undergraduate credits
Tuition $498 for New Jersey residents, $732 for nonresidents
Description   Designed as an intensive one-semester course in world religions, emphasizing specific forms of religious expression and practice.

SOCIOLOGY

Marriage and the Family, OLSOC 210
Prerequisite   None
Credit Value   3 undergraduate credits
Tuition $174 for New Jersey residents, $252 for nonresidents
Description   Provides an understanding of the various approaches to studying the family and the varieties of U.S. family forms and the family life cycle.

U.S. DEPARTMENT OF AGRICULTURE-GRADUATE SCHOOL

Room 1112, South Agriculture Building
14th Street & Independence Avenue, SW
Washington, DC 20250-9911
Telephone: (202) 720-7123
Fax: (202) 720-3603
Web Site: http://grad.usda.gov/corres/corpro.html
E-mail: correspond@grad.usda.gov

Accreditation   See Remarks
Hardware Requirements   Any PC or Macintosh computer with a modem
Software Requirements   Any popular communications software
Remarks   Not a degree-granting institution, the USDA Graduate School has never sought accreditation. Credits awarded by the school are accepted at most colleges and universities.

COMMUNICATIONS

The Internet Made Simple, CCOMM 140
Prerequisite   Introduction to On-Line Communication, CCOMM 115, or a similar course
Credit Value   3 undergraduate credits
Tuition $250
Description   Explores the possibilities of the Internet, and helps students realize how it can aid them in their work, learning, and self-enrichment. Requires a familiarity with bulletin board systems and access to FTP, a Gopher server, and a World Wide Web browser such as Netscape, Mosaic, or Lynx.

Introduction to On-Line Communication, CCOMM 115
Prerequisite   None
Credit Value   2 undergraduate credits

Tuition $160

Description Explains the basics of online communication, including the use of bulletin board systems (BBSs), and develops familiarity with communications software, downloading and uploading from ASCII files, and locating local, free BBS numbers nationwide.

Introduction to Visual Telecommunications, CCOMM 130

Prerequisite None

Credit Value 2 undergraduate credits

Tuition $160

Description Introduces online computer graphics and image transfer. Uses Microsoft® Windows™ Paintbrush and a Macintosh paintbrush program.

UNIVERSITY OF CALIFORNIA EXTENSION

Center for Media and Independent Learning
2000 Center Street, Fourth Floor
Berkeley, CA 94704
Telephone: (510) 642-4124
Fax: (510) 643-9271
Web Site: http://www-cmil.unex.berkeley.edu/
E-mail: cmil@violet.unex.berkeley.edu

Accreditation Western Association of Colleges and Schools

Hardware Requirements Any personal computer with a modem

Software Requirements Most popular communications software will work

Remarks University of California Extension has offered independent learning college courses since 1913. Most courses listed here can be completed through e-mail. A recent innovation has been an arrangement through which some courses can be taken on a more interactive basis through America Online®. These courses are identified by the letters AOL following the description.

ACCOUNTING

Governmental Accounting, X131

Prerequisite Intermediate accounting course or equivalent experience

Credit Value 4 undergraduate credits

Tuition $375

Description Focuses on the preparation of financial statements and the principles and practices common in federal, state, and local government agencies.

ASTRONOMY

Introduction to General Astronomy, XB10
Prerequisite   None
Credit Value   4 undergraduate credits
Tuition $350
Description   An essentially nonmathematical description of modern astronomy with emphasis on the structure and evolution of stars, galaxies, and the universe. Includes discussions of black holes, pulsars, and quasars.

BIOLOGICAL SCIENCES

The Biology of Cancer, X26
Prerequisite   None
Credit Value   3 undergraduate credits
Tuition $350
Description   Examines the fundamental clinical and pathological aspects of the many diseases called cancer from the patient's and health care professional's point of view.

Principles and Techniques of Molecular Cell Biology, X121
Prerequisite   One year of college-level general biology
Credit Value   3 undergraduate credits
Tuition $375
Description   Explains how cells function and how research in cell and molecular biology is making its way out of the laboratory and into everyday life. Topics include cell regulation, genetic engineering and cloning, and the use of DNA technology in forensics.

BOTANY/PLANT SCIENCE

Plant Life in California, X113
Prerequisite   None
Credit Value   3 semester credits
Tuition $375
Description   Focuses on the vegetation, plant communities, and life zones of California, and examines influences on patterns of vegetation and plant distribution throughout the state.

BUSINESS

Career Counseling, 810
Prerequisite   None
Credit Value   Noncredit

Tuition $375

Description A basic course in business management that teaches students how to match their experiences, interests, motivation, and values to a few specific career occupations.

Effective Personnel Administration, X424

Prerequisite None

Credit Value 3 undergraduate credits

Tuition $350

Description Offers a practical guide to becoming an effective personnel administrator capable of influencing the direction, performance, and motivation of employees.

Information Resource Management, X480.6

Prerequisite Basic knowledge of computer information systems and business practices

Credit Value 2 undergraduate credits

Tuition $295

Description An investigation of real-world information system development and implementation, using well-known organizations for case studies.

Introduction to Business Organization and Management, X492.8

Prerequisite None

Credit Value 3 undergraduate credits

Tuition $350

Description Examines the principles and practices used in the operation of both large and small businesses, including the managerial environment, planning, staffing, and motivation.

Introduction to International Business, X192

Prerequisite None

Credit Value 3 undergraduate credits

Tuition $375

Description Examines economic and political considerations relating to international enterprises and how to do business in various cultures.

Investment Management, X430

Prerequisite None

Credit Value 2 undergraduate credits

Tuition $295

Description A comprehensive course covers the investment environment and investment analysis of the securities markets and investment alternatives such as fixed-income and convertible securities.

CIVIL ENGINEERING

Environmental Behavior of Pollutants, X470
Prerequisite   A course in toxicology and risk assessment or its equivalent
Credit Value   2 undergraduate credits
Tuition $380
Description   Examines the release mechanisms and behavior of chemicals in the environment. Useful for environmental professionals involved in the transportation, disposal, or storage of chemicals. Offered via AOL.

Pollution Prevention and Waste Minimization, X472
Prerequisite   Environmental Behavior of Pollutants, X470, or equivalent
Credit Value   2 undergraduate credits
Tuition $380
Description   Presents principles of pollution prevention, waste reduction, and cleaner production processes to reduce chemical and raw material losses. Offered via AOL.

Technologies for Treatment, Disposal, and Remediation of Hazardous Wastes, X417
Prerequisite   Environmental Behavior of Pollutants, X470, or equivalent
Credit Value   2 undergraduate credits
Tuition $380
Description   Provides a practical overview of state-of-the art technologies and future trends in treating and disposal of hazardous wastes. Offered via AOL.

COMPUTER SCIENCE

C Language Programming, X24
Prerequisite   Familiarity with a structured programming language such as Pascal, FORTRAN, COBOL, or Assembler, and access to a programming environment
Credit Value   2 undergraduate credits
Tuition $375
Description   Teaches how to modify existing C language programs and develop auxiliary ones, and discusses the essential structure and function of programs in C.

Concepts of Database Management Systems, X408
Prerequisite   A programming course in any language or equivalent experience
Credit Value   3 undergraduate credits
Tuition $425

Description An in-depth study of the techniques for creating and using database applications, organized around the database life cycle.

Concepts of Information Systems, X42
Prerequisite None
Credit Value 3 undergraduate credits
Tuition $375
Description A general introduction to computer information systems. Topics include computer history, computer applications and their social impact, and career opportunities.

Fundamentals of Data Communications and Networks, X433
Prerequisite None
Credit Value 2 undergraduate credits
Tuition $375
Description Provides practical and current information on data communications concepts and equipment, including modems, DSUs/CSUs, installation procedures, and troubleshooting. Focuses on how equipment and protocols are incorporated into small and large systems.

Fundamentals of C++ Programming, X459
Prerequisite Previous programming experience in a structured language such as C, Pascal, or Modula II
Credit Value 3 undergraduate credits
Tuition $425
Description A hands-on introduction to object-oriented programming using C++, a language designed to make the computer implementation of problem-solving easier, clearer, and more efficient.

Introduction to Programming with BASIC, X11
Prerequisite Concepts of Information Systems, X42, or equivalent experience
Credit Value 3 undergraduate credits
Tuition $375
Description Explains how to use BASIC system commands and program statements, and examines BASIC programming applications.

Introductory Pascal, X13
Prerequisite None
Credit Value 3 undergraduate credits
Tuition $375
Description A hands-on course using Pascal version 7, provides a solid foundation for learning to program in any language.

Systems Analysis and Design: An Overview, X422
Prerequisite   Concepts of Information Systems, X42, or an equivalent course
Credit Value   3 undergraduate credits
Tuition $425
Description   A foundation course, examines information analysis and logical specification of the system development process in an organization, emphasizing the use of analysis and design to meet business objectives. Also available via AOL.

Using the Internet, X43
Prerequisite   None
Credit Value   1 undergraduate credit
Tuition $125
Description   Using CyberWISE software, students learn how to access the information superhighway in this professional-level course, including how to navigate the Internet, use e-mail, surf the World Wide Web, and access online resources.

Using the UNIX Operating System, X415
Prerequisite   Access to a UNIX system
Credit Value   3 undergraduate credits
Tuition $425
Description   A comprehensive introduction to the UNIX operating system, designed for programmers and users who wish to add an understanding of UNIX to their skills.

ECONOMICS

Introduction to Macroeconomics, X3
Prerequisite   None
Credit Value   3 undergraduate credits
Tuition $350
Description   An introduction to economic analysis and policy; covers the market economy, government and the economy, and money and banking, among other topics.

ENVIRONMENTAL STUDIES

Careers in Environmental Management, 820
Prerequisite   None
Credit Value   Noncredit
Tuition $95
Description   Designed for individuals who are interested in entering the environmental management field as well as for professionals in the field who may be considering a job or career change. Available via AOL.

Environmental Auditing and Assessment, X473
Prerequisite None
Credit Value 2 undergraduate credits
Tuition $380
Description Offers a descriptive overview of the techniques and processes in conducting environmental audits and assessments, focusing on their use as management tools. Available via AOL.

Environmental Issues, XB10
Prerequisite None
Credit Value 4 undergraduate credits
Tuition $350
Description Studies the relationship between human society and the natural environment, and examines cases of ecosystem maintenance and disruption.

Environmental Regulatory Framework, X488
Prerequisite Principles of Hazardous Materials Management, X123
Credit Value 2 undergraduate credits
Tuition $380
Description Examines the regulatory framework governing hazardous substances from production to disposal, emphasizing the federal, state, and local laws, regulations, and rules as well as the agencies charged with enforcing them. Available via AOL.

Hazardous Materials Emergency Management, X490
Prerequisite A course in environmental behavior of pollutants
Credit Value 2 undergraduate credits
Tuition $380
Description Teaches the emergency management process, including prevention and mitigation, preparedness, response, and recovery. Available via AOL.

Principles of Hazardous Materials Management, X123
Prerequisite None
Credit Value 2 undergraduate credits
Tuition $380
Description Surveys the scientific, regulatory, and sociopolitical aspects of hazardous materials management. Discusses hazard definitions, management of risks during production, storage and transportation, management of hazardous waste, and personal protection and safety. Available via AOL.

Toxicology & Risk Assessment for Environmental Decision Making, X489
Prerequisite Environmental Regulatory Framework, X488
Credit Value 2 undergraduate credits

Tuition $380

Description Examines the toxic effects hazardous chemicals have on biological systems, including dose–response curves, mechanisms of toxicity, carcinogens, and reproductive hazards. Available via AOL.

FILM

The Art of Film History, X20
Prerequisite None
Credit Value 3 undergraduate credits
Tuition $375
Description Explores the techniques of evaluating and appreciating films. Topics include the handling of space and time in motion pictures, the history and uses of sound, editing, and directing. Also available via AOL.

GEOLOGY

Earthquakes: Their Geology and Human Impact, X2
Prerequisite None
Credit Value 1 undergraduate credit
Tuition $125
Description Covers plate tectonics, the nature of faults, the causes, characteristics, and effects of earthquakes, and issues of public safety.

LITERATURE

American Fiction, XD158B
Prerequisite None
Credit Value 4 undergraduate quarter credits
Tuition $350
Description A survey of major American authors from the turn of the century to the present, including Crane, Wharton, Fitzgerald, Hemingway, Faulkner, and Kesey.

Multicultural Literature, X55
Prerequisite None
Credit Value 3 undergraduate credits
Tuition $350
Description Highlights the rich diversity of American culture in general and of American literature in particular.

MANAGEMENT

Quality Management, X470.9
Prerequisite None

Credit Value 2 undergraduate credits
Tuition $295
Description Provides a comprehensive foundation for understanding total quality management, what it is, and how to implement it throughout an organization. Topics include organizational development, group communications, human resources, and analytical tools.

MARKETING

Principles of Marketing, X463.3
Prerequisite None
Credit Value 3 undergraduate credits
Tuition $375
Description Covers marketing's role in business decision-making, market segmentation, consumer buying behavior, and marketing's effect on company image and profitabilty.

MATHEMATICS

Introduction to Statistics, XB2
Prerequisite High school algebra
Credit Value 4 undergraduate credits
Tuition $395
Description Examines population and variables and standard measures of location, spread, and association. Topics also include normal approximation, probability and sampling, binomial distribution, and regression.

NUTRITION

The New Nutrition, X107
Prerequisite None
Credit Value 2 undergraduate credits
Tuition $250
Description Explores the frontiers of nutritional science, with the goal of demystifying healthy eating. Provides current information about diet and nutrition in terms of individual life-styles, inherited risks, tastes, and needs at all stages of life.

Nutrition, X103
Prerequisite High school or introductory college-level chemistry, biology, or physiology
Credit Value 3 undergraduate credits
Tuition $375
Description Discusses essential nutrients and their functions in the human

body. Also examines the effects of nutrients on tissues, nutrient requirements in various stages of human development, and the nutrient content of foods.

PHILOSOPHY

History of Western Philosophy, X20A
Prerequisite   None
Credit Value   3 undergraduate credits
Tuition $375
Description   Covers the pre-Socratic period to the end of the Middle Ages. Introduces major philosophical concerns and concepts in Western thought, and explores philosophical questions relating to politics, metaphysics, natural science, logic, and ethics.

PHYSICAL EDUCATION/HEALTH

Community Responses to Alcohol & Other Drug Problems, X180
Prerequisite   A course on alcohol and other drug problems
Credit Value   2 undergraduate credits
Description   Studies the broad range of community responses to alcohol and other drug problems, including prevention policies of government, business, and labor institutions.

The Modern Plague: HIV and AIDS, X177
Prerequisite   None
Credit Value   1 undergraduate credit
Tuition $125
Description   Traces the HIV infection from its earliest recognition in a few isolated cases less than two decades ago to the worldwide epidemic today. Examines risk factors, risk groups, prevention, and treatment.

POLITICAL SCIENCE

American Institutions, XB100
Prerequisite   None
Credit Value   3 undergraduate credits
Tuition $375
Description   Examines the basic workings of the U.S. Constitution and the institutions of the federal government, the American system of electoral politics, and areas of public policy.

PSYCHOLOGY

Abnormal Psychology, XL127
Prerequisite   None

Credit Value   4 undergraduate quarter credits
Tuition $375
Description   Covers the dynamics and prevention of abnormal behavior, including neuroses, psychoses, character disorders, psychosomatic reactions, and schizophrenia.

Adolescence, X139.1
Prerequisite   None
Credit Value   3 undergraduate credits
Tuition $375
Description   Examines adolescents' physical, mental, emotional, social, and personality characteristics and current theories about them.

Critical Thinking, X23
Prerequisite   None
Credit Value   3 undergraduate credits
Tuition $350
Description   Teaches strategies for learning how to learn and for critical and creative thinking, including complex problem-solving. Examines why people think the way they do. Also available via AOL.

Developmental Psychology, XL130
Prerequisite   A course in general psychology and an introduction to statistics course
Credit Value   4 undergraduate quarter credits
Tuition $375
Description   Provides overview of child development, including prenatal development, birth, and the newborn, and physical, cognitive, language, emotional, and social development.

Psychology of Communication, X156.1
Prerequisite   Junior standing
Credit Value   3 undergraduate credits
Tuition $375
Description   Focuses on why people communicate the way they do and how they can communicate better. Considers the practical applications of theory and research to personal and professional communication. Also available via AOL.

RELIGION

Views of the Absolute in World Religions, X10
Prerequisite   None
Credit Value   3 undergraduate credits

Tuition $375

Description   Explores a variety of world religions, focusing on their definitions of the Absolute and how the individual relates to it.

SOCIOLOGY

Principles of Sociology: A Multicultural Perspective, X2
Prerequisite   None
Credit Value   3 undergraduate credits
Tuition $350
Description   An introductory course focusing on the basic topics, concepts, and principles of the discipline. Considers the influence of social phenomena on human behavior using comparative multicultural and cross-cultural approaches.

WRITING

Technical Writing, X412
Prerequisite   None
Credit Value   3 undergraduate credits
Tuition $375
Description   Develops your ability to organize information into manuals, journal articles, reports, and other technical publications. Also covers document design and production principles, computerized "interactive" documentation, and taking your publication to press.

Writing Fundamentals, 804
Prerequisite   None
Credit Value   Noncredit
Tuition $325
Description   Helps master the basics of writing clear, grammatically correct sentences and effective paragraphs.

Writing a Successful Essay, 800
Prerequisite   None
Credit Value   1 undergraduate credit
Tuition $125
Description   Designed for anyone who needs to refresh or improve essay writing skills, this course provides an understanding of the writing process and the essay form, and reviews essential writing skills.

UNIVERSITY OF ILLINOIS AT URBANA-CHAMPAIGN

Division of Guided Individual Study
Office of Continuing Education

Suite 1406, 302 East John Street
Champaign, IL 61820
Telephone: (217) 333-1321
Web Site: http://www.extramural.uiuc.edu/
E-mail: gisinfo@c3po.uiuc.edu

Accreditation   North Central Association of Colleges and Schools
Hardware Requirements   Any IBM-compatible computer with an Internet connection
Software Requirements   Requires purchase of Mathematica software
Remarks   This state university also offers a wide variety of correspondence-based independent study courses for full credit.

COMMUNICATIONS

Using the Internet: A Tool Kit, Info Tech n100
Prerequisite   None
Credit Value   Noncredit
Tuition $148
Description   Explores the tools for using the information superhighway, the Internet: electronic mail, Telnet, file transfer protocol (FTP), Gopher, World Wide Web, NCSA Mosaic, Netscape, and more.

MATHEMATICS

Advanced Calculus, Math X280
Prerequisite   Math X242C or Math X245C
Credit Value   3 undergraduate credits
Tuition $328
Description   An introductory study of vector calculus and functions of several variables. Topics include directional derivatives, maxima and minima, and line and surface integrals.

Calculus, Math X135C
Prerequisite   A course in plane or analytic geometry or equivalent
Credit Value   5 undergraduate credits
Tuition $400
Description   A first course in calculus, discusses differentiation and integration and applications to curve-tracing, area, and volume.

Calculus II, Math X245C
Prerequisite   Math X135C
Credit Value   5 undergraduate credits
Tuition $400

Extramural Programs and Guided Individual Study WWW Server

Welcome to the World Wide Web Server of the Department of Extramural Programs and Guided Individual Study (GIS), of the University of Illinois at Urbana-Champaign. You will find here general information about Extramural Programs and GIS, policies, departmental staff information, as well as course descriptions, timetables, and enrollment procedures.

- **Extramural Programs**

- **Guided Individual Study (Correspondence Courses)**

- **Distance Learning**

- **Internet Courses**

Other Web Documents:
- Visit the College of Agriculture Discovery System
- NCSA's Starting Points for Internet Exploration
- Other Big-10 WWW Servers
- UIUC Continuing Education and Public Service WWW Server
- The Prairienet WWW Server (the Free-Net of East-Central Illinois)

 Future Ideas for *www.extramural.uiuc.edu*

 Usage statistics for *www.extramural.uiuc.edu*

About this machine. *www.extramural.uiuc.edu*

Description   A continuation of Math X135C, focuses on polar coordinates, vectors and parametric equations, infinite series, and multiple integrals.

Calculus and Analytical Geometry, Math X242C
Prerequisite   An introductory course in calculus and analytical geometry
Credit Value   3 undergraduate credits
Tuition $256
Description   An advanced course, focuses on geometry of space, partial differentiation, and multiple integrals.

Differential Equations and Orthogonal Functions, Math X285C
Prerequisite   Math X242C or equivalent
Credit Value   3 undergraduate credits
Tuition $256
Description   Intended for engineering students and others who require a working knowledge of differential equations, this course covers techniques and applications.

UNIVERSITY OF IOWA COLLEGE OF EDUCATION

Guided Correspondence Study
116 International Center
Iowa City, IA 52242-1802
Telephone: (319) 335-2575 or (800) 272-6430
Fax: (319) 335-2740
Web Site: http://www.uiowa.edu/~ccp/
E-mail: credit-programs@uiowa.edu

Accreditation   North Central Association of Colleges and Schools
Hardware Requirements   Any personal computer with a modem and Internet connection
Software Requirements   Any popular communications software
Remarks   The university plans to add more of its independent study courses to the following ones, which are the only Internet-based courses currently available.

HISTORY

First World War, 16E:185
Prerequisite   None
Credit Value   3 undergraduate credits
Tuition $237
Description   Examines the war from military, cultural, and social points of

view, and assesses the impact of the war on diverse groups of people and on Western culture.

LITERATURE

Science Fiction (Historical Survey), 8:182
Prerequisite None
Credit Value 3 undergraduate credits
Tuition $237
Description An historical survey of science fiction, beginning with Shelley's *Frankenstein,* followed by the works of H. G. Wells and a look at the genre over the last fifty years.

SOCIOLOGY

Introduction to Sociology: Principles, 34:1
Prerequisite None
Credit Value 3 undergraduate credits
Tuition $237
Description Examines how individuals are organized into social groups, ranging from intimate groups to bureaucracies, and how these influence individual behavior.

UNIVERSITY OF MARYLAND UNIVERSITY COLLEGE

Open Learning
University Boulevard at Adelphi Road
College Park, MD 20742–1660
Telephone: (301) 985-7000 or (800) 283-6832
Fax: (301) 985-4615
E-mail: open-learning@listserv.umuc.edu

Accreditation Middle States Association of Colleges and Schools
Hardware Requirements Any PC or Macintosh computer with a modem
Software Requirements Appropriate software included as part of the tuition for these courses
Remarks The university offers an external bachelor's degree program for those seeking a degree without attending classes.

BEHAVIORAL SCIENCES

Introduction to Research Methods and Statistics, BEHS 202
Prerequisite College algebra or equivalent
Credit Value 3 undergraduate credits

Tuition $522 for Maryland residents, $585 for nonresidents

Description   An introduction to research in the social sciences, emphasizing the role of statistical analysis in answering questions. Topics include the measurement of variables, methods of designing questionnaires, and data coding.

Risk, BEHS 444

Prerequisite   None

Credit Value   6 undergraduate credits

Tuition $1,044 for Maryland residents, $1,170 for nonresidents

Description   An interdisciplinary analysis of risk, drawing on literature in the social sciences and management. Topics include calculations of risk, recognition of the risks inherent in decisions, and risk analysis in public policy.

BUSINESS

Business Analysis Methods, MGMT 316

Prerequisite   A basic math course or equivalent

Credit Value   3 undergraduate credits

Tuition $522 for Maryland residents, $585 for nonresidents

Description   An examination of the sources and uses of information in an organization. Topics include methods of research, statistical procedures, and models used in forecasting.

The Business/Government Relationship, TMGT 340

Prerequisite   None

Credit Value   6 undergraduate credits

Tuition $1,044 for Maryland residents, $1,170 for nonresidents

Description   Assesses the business/government relationship as important because the largest corporations and the government dominate the nation's economic and political life. Topics include antitrust, transportation, and the environment.

COMMUNICATIONS

Writing for Managers, COMM 390

Prerequisite   English 101 or equivalent

Credit Value   3 undergraduate credits

Tuition $522 for Maryland residents, $585 for nonresidents

Description   Discusses the kinds of writing skills managers need for the workplace, including effectively organizing information, writing for a specific purpose and audience, mastering the mechanics of written English, and evaluating one's own writing.

COMPUTER SCIENCE

Computer Networking, CMSC 440
Prerequisite CMSC 370
Credit Value 3 undergraduate credits
Tuition $522 for Maryland residents, $585 for nonresidents
Description An investigation of networks and their components. Includes local area networks, wide area networks, interconnection, and internetworking.

Data Communications, CMSC 370
Prerequisite Contact the university
Credit Value 3 undergraduate credits
Tuition $522 for Maryland residents, $585 for nonresidents
Description An examination of the impact of data communication and its components based primarily on the open systems interconnection (or OSI) model.

Distributed Systems, CMSC 445
Prerequisite Knowledge of networking and the programming language C.
Credit Value 3 undergraduate credits
Tuition $522 for Maryland residents, $585 for nonresidents
Description An examination of concepts and techniques for implementing applications in a distributed computing environment.

CULTURAL STUDIES

Crossing Cultures: World Views in the Humanities, HUMN 301
Prerequisite None
Credit Value 6 undergraduate credits
Tuition $1,044 for Maryland residents, $1,170 for nonresidents
Description An examination of Western and non-Western roots of human identity viewed from philosophical, cultural, and intellectual perspectives.

MANAGEMENT

Human-Resources Management, TMGT 360
Prerequisite None
Credit Value 6 undergraduate credits
Tuition $1,044 for Maryland residents, $1,170 for nonresidents
Description An examination of the role of human resources in the life of an organization, including such topics as total quality management and traditional functions of a human resources manager.

Management: Perspectives, Process, Productivity, TMGT 302
Prerequisite   None
Credit Value   6 undergraduate credits
Tuition $1,044 for Maryland residents, $1,170 for nonresidents
Description   A systematic exploration of management processes and organizational behavior. Topics include planning, leading, group dynamics, and motivation.

Management in a Global Context, TMGT 390
Prerequisite   None
Credit Value   6 undergraduate credits
Tuition $1,044 for Maryland residents, $1,170 for nonresidents
Description   A survey of international business management in the context of the increasing economic interdependence of nations. Foreign techniques of management are explored.

Managerial Planning and Competitive Strategies, MGMT 495
Prerequisite   Introductory management courses
Credit Value   3 undergraduate credits
Tuition $522 for Maryland residents, $585 for nonresidents
Description   An overview of the continuous, systematic process of managerial planning, including environmental scanning and the development of plans and strategies to gain competitive advantage.

Managing in the Public Sector, TMGT 305
Prerequisite   None
Credit Value   6 undergraduate credits
Tuition $1,044 for Maryland residents, $1,170 for nonresidents
Description   Explores the nature of public sector management, including issues of public accountability, the budgetary process, and personnel.

Organization Development, TMGT 350
Prerequisite   None
Credit Value   6 undergraduate credits
Tuition $1,044 for Maryland residents, $1,170 for nonresidents
Description   Introduces a method of making organizations and individuals more adaptive and productive. Techniques of intervention such as team building, process consultation, and conflict resolution are explained.

Organizational Communication, MGMT 320
Prerequisite   A basic course in leadership and management
Credit Value   3 undergraduate credits
Tuition $522 for Maryland residents, $585 for nonresidents
Description   A study of the structure of communication in organizations.

Problems, issues, and techniques of organizational communication are analyzed in case histories.

Problem Solving, TMGT 310
Prerequisite   None
Credit Value   6 undergraduate credits
Tuition $1,044 for Maryland residents, $1,170 for nonresidents
Description   Discusses the theoretical and practical aspects of strategies used in solving problems, an activity that takes up much of a manager's day. Case studies are used to illustrate the definition of the problem, the formulation of a hypothesis, and the collection and analysis of data.

Project Management, TMGT 430
Prerequisite   None
Credit Value   6 undergraduate credits
Tuition $1,044 for Maryland residents, $1,170 for nonresidents
Description   Presents management of projects as a means of production in research firms and high-technology manufacturing and engineering firms. The practical considerations of designing a project management system are included.

Strategic Management, TMGT 380
Prerequisite   None
Credit Value   6 undergraduate credits
Tuition $1,044 for Maryland residents, $1,170 for nonresidents
Description   Explores the continuous and systematic process of planning and implementing strategic decisions. Topics covered include definition of mission, analysis of issues, formulation of strategy, and implementation and control of policies.

Total Quality Management, MGMT 425
Prerequisite   Business Analysis Methods, MGMT 316
Credit Value   3 undergraduate credits
Tuition $522 for Maryland residents, $585 for nonresidents
Description   A survey of methods used to apply total quality management in various organizational settings to improve quality and productivity. Models, tools, and techniques are discussed.

MARKETING

Principles of Marketing, MGMT 322
Prerequisite   None
Credit Value   3 undergraduate credits
Tuition $522 for Maryland residents, $585 for nonresidents

Description   An overview of the field of marketing, with special attention to marketing research, consumer behavior, and marketing strategies. Includes services and nonprofit marketing as well as international marketing.

MATHEMATICS

Mathematics: Contemporary Topics & Applications, MATH 105
Prerequisite   None
Credit Value   3 undergraduate credits
Tuition $522 for Maryland residents, $585 for nonresidents
Description   A survey of contemporary topics in mathematics, centering on applications and projects. Topics include measurements, rates of growth, basic statistics, and the math of political power.

UNIVERSITY OF MINNESOTA

Department of Independent and Distance Learning
45 Wesbrook Hall, 77 Pleasant Street, SE
Minneapolis, MN 55455-0216
Telephone: (612) 624-0000 or (800) 234-6564
Fax: (612) 626-7900
Web Site: http://www.cee.umn.edu/dis/
E-mail: indstudy@maroon.tc.umn.edu/dis/
Gopher Hole: gopher://mail.cee.umn.edu:70/11/dis

Accreditation   North Central Association of Colleges and Schools
Hardware Requirements   Any personal computer with communications capability
Software Requirements   Any popular communications software
Remarks   The courses listed here, as well as several hundred more, are also available as correspondence-based independent study college courses.

AFRO-AMERICAN/AFRICAN STUDIES

Introduction to African Literature, AFRO 3601
Prerequisite   None
Credit Value   4 undergraduate quarter credits
Tuition $344
Description   A survey of nineteenth- and twentieth-century African litera-ture, including oral narratives, written poetry, short stories, novels, and plays.

AMERICAN INDIAN STUDIES

American Indian History I, AMIN 3111
Prerequisite None
Credit Value 4 undergraduate quarter credits
Tuition $344
Description Explores Native American history from the mid-fifteenth century to 1850, addressing themes related to various cultures and how they changed when they came into contact with other Native American groups and with Europeans.

American Indian History II, AMIN 3112
Prerequisite None; AMIN 3111 is not required
Credit Value 4 undergraduate quarter credits
Tuition $344
Description Covers Native American history from 1850 to the present, and explores the tensions between Native American and European American cultures.

AMERICAN STUDIES

American Cultures II, AMST 1002
Prerequisite None
Credit Value 4 undergraduate quarter credits
Tuition $318
Description An interdisciplinary study of the diversity of American cultures. Covers the period between 1890 and 1945. Major topics include urban life and leisure, changing family and gender roles, and race and national identity.

American Cultures III, AMST 1002
Prerequisite None; American Cultures II is not required
Credit Value 4 undergraduate quarter credits
Tuition $318
Description An interdisciplinary study of the diversity of American cultures. Covers the period from 1945 to the present. Major topics include social change movements, the politics of popular culture, and family practices and gender roles.

Ellery Queen & the American Detective Story, AMST 1920
Prerequisite None
Credit Value 4 undergraduate quarter credits
Tuition $318
Description Surveys American detective fiction to suggest reasons for its continued popularity. Discussed are the works of Poe, Hammett, Stout, and others in addition to Queen.

ANTHROPOLOGY

Human Origins, ANTH 1101
Prerequisite None
Credit Value 5 undergraduate quarter credits
Tuition $397.50
Description Examines world prehistory as investigated by archaeologists, including their methods and concepts in the study of human origins.

ART

Introduction to the Visual Arts, ARTH 1001
Prerequisite None
Credit Value 4 undergraduate quarter credits
Tuition $318
Description Considers the basic issues of art. Examples of painting and sculpture are analyzed to illustrate the roles of art in society.

BIOLOGICAL SCIENCES

Heredity and Human Society, BIOL 1101
Prerequisite None
Credit Value 4 undergraduate quarter credits
Tuition $318
Description Reviews the principles of heredity and their social and cultural implications. Explains the use and misuse of genetics and the relationships between genetics, evolution, and individual and social behavior.

BUSINESS

Business & Society: Ethics and Stakeholder Management, BGS 3002
Prerequisite None
Credit Value 4 undergraduate quarter credits
Tuition $374
Description Discusses business as an institution and its relationships to other institutions in society. Includes an examination of the ethical and practical conflicts in the role of the firm and the manager in the context of the public policy process.

COMMUNICATIONS

Interneting for Biologists and Others, FSCN 5111
Prerequisite None

Credit Value 3 undergraduate quarter credits

Tuition $280.50

Description Discusses the skills needed to get the most out of the Internet. Subjects include static resources such as Gopher and Mosaic, dynamic interaction (IRC and MOOs), and electronic mail and newsgroups.

CULTURAL STUDIES

Discourse and Society I: Reading Culture, CSCL 1301

Prerequisite None

Credit Value 4 undergraduate quarter credits

Tuition $318

Description Prepares students to think, write, and speak critically about different forms of cultural production by studying art, literature, mass media, social history, and cultural theory.

Discourse and Society II: Meaning and History, CSCL 1302

Prerequisite None

Credit Value 4 undergraduate quarter credits

Tuition $318

Description Examines historically grounded case studies—early eighteenth-century art, two novels, a historical work, an anthropological work, an opera, and others. Students relate the discourses in the case studies to the socio-historical conditions out of which they arose.

EDUCATION

Creating Social Studies Curriculum, EDUC 5666

Prerequisite None

Credit Value 3 undergraduate quarter credits

Tuition $280.50

Description Uses historic sites and related materials to create new social studies curricula. Implements and evaluates living history learning experiences in the classroom.

Directed Study: Inventing the Future, EDPA 5099

Prerequisite None

Credit Value 4 undergraduate quarter credits

Tuition $374

Description Covers trends in work, leisure, education, technology, health, spirituality, and home life.

Second Languages and Young Children, CI 5620

Prerequisite None

Credit Value 4 undergraduate quarter credits

Tuition $374

Description Examines current approaches to teaching second languages to young children, with emphasis on innovative curricular models. Provides information on the way young children acquire language and the effects of bilingualism on child development.

ENGLISH

Twentieth Century English Novel, ENGL 5153
Prerequisite None
Credit Value 4 undergraduate quarter credits
Tuition $344
Description A study of the British novel of the twentieth century, emphasizing some of its main ideas, techniques, and relationships to the history of the novel. Authors include Forster, Joyce, Lawrence, Waugh, Woolf, and Murdoch.

ENTOMOLOGY

Principles of Beekeeping, ENT 3020
Prerequisite None
Credit Value 4 undergraduate quarter credits
Tuition $374
Description Useful to both inexperienced and experienced beekeepers, covers the history of beekeeping, life history and behavior of honeybees, colony and apiary management, pollination and hive products, and honeybee diseases and their control.

ENVIRONMENTAL STUDIES

Conservation of Natural Resources, FR 1201
Prerequisite None
Credit Value 3 undergraduate quarter credits
Tuition $238.50
Description Discusses current status, utilization, and sound management of natural resources, with emphasis on the ecological approach. Topics include the application of conservation principles to soil, water, forests, grasslands, wildlife, minerals, and energy sources.

HISTORY

American Constitutional History I, HIST 5331
Prerequisite None
Credit Value 4 undergraduate quarter credits
Tuition $344

Description Covers the origins and development of constitutional government in the United States with emphasis on the role of constitutional politics in the evolution of public policy. Covers the colonial period through Reconstruction.

American Constitutional History II, HIST 5332
Prerequisite None
Credit Value 4 undergraduate quarter credits
Tuition $344
Description Emphasizes the Constitution and the rule of law in modern America, from the Reconstruction to the present.

American History I, HIST 1301
Prerequisite None
Credit Value 5 undergraduate quarter credits
Tuition $397.50
Description Covers U.S. history from colonial times through the Reconstruction, including political, economic, social, and diplomatic history. Major topics include the Salem witchcraft trials, the American Revolution, and the Civil War.

American History II, HIST 1302
Prerequisite None
Credit Value 5 undergraduate quarter credits
Tuition $397.50
Description Covers U.S. history from 1880 to the present. Major topics include the rise of industrial America, various reform movements, both world wars, the Depression, the Vietnam War, and the Reagan years.

Civil War and Reconstruction, HIST 3812
Prerequisite None
Credit Value 4 undergraduate quarter credits
Tuition $344
Description Integrates scholarly readings with the Ken Burns PBS series *The Civil War.* Major topics include the military aspects of the war, politics and society from 1848 to 1877, sectional differences, slavery and emancipation, and Reconstruction politics.

History of American Foreign Relations 1760–1865, HIST 3881
Prerequisite None
Credit Value 4 undergraduate quarter credits
Tuition $344
Description Covers foreign policy and diplomacy during the period of independence and territorial expansion. Topics include diplomacy during

the American Revolution, the War of 1812, the Civil War, the Mexican War, and the Monroe Doctrine.

History of American Foreign Relations 1945–1995, HIST 3883
Prerequisite   None
Credit Value   4 undergraduate quarter credits
Tuition $344
Description   Examines foreign policy from the end of World War II through the Vietnam War, the Reagan presidency, and the fall of Communism.

Introduction to Modern European History 1, HIST 1001
Prerequisite   None
Credit Value   4 undergraduate quarter credits
Tuition $318
Description   Surveys European history from the Middle Ages to the eighteenth century, with emphasis on the rise of the nation-state and the role of Christianity and exploration in its development.

Introduction to Modern European History 2, HIST 1002
Prerequisite   None
Credit Value   4 undergraduate credits
Tuition $318
Description   Surveys European history during the eighteenth and nineteenth centuries, with emphasis on the struggle for control of the state, the Age of Reason, and the French Revolution.

Introduction to Modern European History 3, HIST 1003
Prerequisite   None
Credit Value   4 undergraduate quarter credits
Tuition $318
Description   Surveys European history during the eighteenth and nineteenth centuries, with emphasis on the impact of industrialization and the two world wars.

Survey of Civilizations in Ancient Asia, HIST 1451
Prerequisite   None
Credit Value   4 undergraduate quarter credits
Tuition $318
Description   Examines ancient societies, political systems, religions, and cultures of East, South, and West Asia.

Sweden: 1560–1721, HIST 3700
Prerequisite   None

Credit Value   4 undergraduate quarter credits
Tuition $344
Description   Studies the formation and dismantling of Sweden's Baltic empire between 1560 and 1721. Highlights the administrative, economic, and social foundations of the experience.

The United States in the 20th Century, HIST 3822
Prerequisite   None
Credit Value   4 undergraduate quarter credits
Tuition $344
Description   Covers the Great Depression, the coming of World War II, the origins of the Cold War, the Eisenhower era, the civil rights movement, and labor relations.

JOURNALISM

Communication and Public Opinion, JOUR 5501
Prerequisite   None
Credit Value   4 undergraduate quarter credits
Tuition $344
Description   Includes theories of mass communication, models of the communication process, and research on public opinion and persuasion.

LANGUAGES

Beginning Latin I, LAT 1101
Prerequisite   None
Credit Value   5 undergraduate quarter credits
Tuition $397.50
Description   Includes basic grammar and vocabulary, practice in reading and writing Latin, workbook exercises, easy Latin readings, and Roman legends.

Beginning Latin II, LAT 1102
Prerequisite   LAT 1101
Credit Value   5 undergraduate quarter credits
Tuition $397.50
Description   Continues from LAT 1101.

Selections from Latin Literature, LAT 1103
Prerequisite   LAT 1102
Credit Value   5 undergraduate quarter credits
Tuition $397.50
Description   A review and expansion of the previous two courses, LAT

1101 and LAT 1102, with a considerable amount of historical and literary background.

Latin Prose and Poetry, LAT 1104
Prerequisite LAT 1103 or equivalent
Credit Value 5 undergraduate quarter credits
Tuition $397.50
Description Includes selections from Caesar, Cicero, Livy, and others.

Latin Poetry: Vergil's Aeneid, LAT 3106
Prerequisite LAT 1103 or equivalent
Credit Value 5 undergraduate quarter credits
Tuition $430
Description Includes readings of selections from Books I and II; background about Roman life and thought is included in the text.

MANAGEMENT

Entrepreneurship & the Small Enterprise, MGMT 3008
Prerequisite Instructor's consent
Credit Value 4 undergraduate quarter credits
Tuition $374
Description Assesses opportunities and constraints in establishing and managing one's own firm, including structuring a new venture, buying into an existing enterprise, and other options.

Fundamentals of Management, MGMT 3001
Prerequisite Completion of 90 credits
Credit Value 4 undergraduate quarter credits
Tuition $374
Description Examines leadership and management functions such as those required to establish goals, policies, procedures, and plans. Topics include motivation, planning and control systems, and concepts of organizational behavior.

MUSIC

The Avant-Garde, MUS 3045
Prerequisite None
Credit Value 4 undergraduate quarter credits
Tuition $344
Description Centers on composers of the American musical avant-garde, circa 1950–1970, including John Cage and Pauline Oliveras, in their sonic and social contexts.

20th Century American Music, MUS 5702
Prerequisite   None
Credit Value   4 undergraduate quarter credits
Tuition $344
Description   Analyzes American music during the twentieth century: folk, popular, classical, Black and Chicano, opera and symphony, and contemporary.

NURSING

Life Span Growth and Development I, NURS 3690
Prerequisite   A general psychology and a general biology course
Credit Value   2 undergraduate quarter credits
Tuition $187
Description   An introductory course, incorporating biological, sociological, and psychological perspectives of human life-span development from conception through adolescence.

Life Span Growth and Development II, NURS 3691
Prerequisite   NURS 3690 or equivalent
Credit Value   2 undergraduate quarter credits
Tuition $187
Description   A continuation of NURS 3690, extending from adolescence through aging and the death experience.

PHILOSOPHY

Introduction to Philosophy, PHIL 1002
Prerequisite   None
Credit Value   5 undergraduate quarter credits
Tuition $397.50
Description   Traces the history of Western philosophy through the works of Plato, Descartes, Hume, Kant, Wittgenstein, and Kuhn.

POLITICAL SCIENCE

American Government and Politics, POL 1001
Prerequisite   None
Credit Value   5 undergraduate quarter credits
Tuition $397.50
Description   An introduction to the ways in which the goals of political actors and the structures of government combine to influence U.S. national policy-making. Includes two case studies of recent events in U.S. politics.

American Political Parties, POL 5737
Prerequisite   POL 1001
Credit Value   4 undergraduate quarter credits
Tuition $344
Description   Examines the activities of political parties in the United States, including recruiting, nominating candidates, and campaigning. Other topics include reform movements, third parties, and independents.

Judicial Process, POL 3309
Prerequisite   POL 1001 or equivalent
Credit Value   4 undergraduate quarter credits
Tuition $344
Description   A study of the structure of the U.S. judiciary branch, including the selection of judges, the process of litigation, influences on judicial decisions, and the role of the Supreme Court.

The United States Congress, POL 3308
Prerequisite   None
Credit Value   4 undergraduate quarter credits
Tuition $344
Description   An examination of the U.S. Congress's internal organization, committee system, party leadership, legislative policy-making, relationship with the president and the bureaucracy, and the various influences on its members.

PSYCHOLOGY

Adolescent Psychology, CPSY 5303
Prerequisite   5 credits of introductory psychology
Credit Value   4 undergraduate quarter credits
Tuition $374
Description   A survey of the behavior and psychological development of the adolescent, including biological factors, cognition and creativity, moral development, ego identity, and sexual development.

Infancy, CPSY 3302
Prerequisite   An introductory child psychology course
Credit Value   4 undergraduate quarter credits
Tuition $374
Description   An examination of the perceptual, motor, emotional, social, and cognitive development during the first two years of life.

Introduction to Child Psychology, CPSY 1301
Prerequisite   5 credits of introductory psychology

Credit Value   4 undergraduate quarter credits
Tuition $318
Description   Designed to provide an understanding of children and their development, the methods used by child psychologists, and the critical evaluation of research.

Introduction to Social Development, CPSY 3331
Prerequisite   CPSY 1301
Credit Value   4 undergraduate quarter credits
Tuition $374
Description   A study of the processes of individual change from infancy through adolescence and the development of capacities for and influences of social relations.

RELIGION

Religions of East Asia, RELS 1032
Prerequisite   None
Credit Value   4 undergraduate quarter credits
Tuition $318
Description   A survey of the religious traditions of China and Japan, exploring beliefs and practices from antiquity to modern times. Includes elements of Taoism, Confucianism, Buddhism, and Shintoism.

RUSSIAN

Russian Literature: Middle Ages–Dostoevsky, RUSS 3421
Prerequisite   None
Credit Value   4 undergraduate quarter credits
Tuition $344
Description   Covers the history of Russian literature from its beginnings around 1000 A.D. to the middle of the nineteenth century. Included are Pushkin, Gogol, and Dostoevsky.

SOCIAL WORK

Introduction to American Social Welfare and Community Services, SW 1001
Prerequisite   None
Credit Value   5 undergraduate quarter credits
Tuition $397.50
Description   A survey of social services and their components, including fields of practice, multiple auspices, levels of participation, and differing ideologies.

SOCIOLOGY

Sociology and Social Problems, SOC 1100
Prerequisite   None
Credit Value   5 undergraduate quarter credits
Tuition $397.50
Description   An introduction to the process by which sociological theories are developed and tested, showing how those theories may be applied usefully to major social problems.

Women in Muslim Society, SOC 3340
Prerequisite   None
Credit Value   5 undergraduate quarter credits
Tuition $430
Description   An introduction to the role of women in Muslim society from a sociological perspective, including their status and roles.

STATISTICS

Introduction to Ideas of Statistics, STAT 1001
Prerequisite   High school algebra
Credit Value   4 undergraduate quarter credits
Tuition $318
Description   A survey of statistical ideas that emphasizes concepts over computation. Includes controlled versus observational studies, sampling, and accuracy of estimates.

WRITING

Technical Writing for Engineers, COMP 3031
Prerequisite   An introductory writing course or equivalent
Credit Value   4 undergraduate quarter credits
Tuition $344
Description   Emphasizing the writing process, this course helps students learn about technical writing for different audiences and ways to achieve it.

Writing about Literature, COMP 3011
Prerequisite   An introductory writing course or equivalent
Credit Value   4 undergraduate quarter credits
Tuition $344
Description   Examines and makes use of different modes of explication and criticism, and develops a critical argument about literary texts with attention to the use of secondary sources.

Writing about Science, COMP 3015
Prerequisite An introductory writing course or equivalent
Credit Value 4 undergraduate quarter credits
Tuition $344
Description Designed to improve the ability of students interested in science, and writing for science, this course discusses various tasks and forms of science writing.

Writing for the Arts, COMP 3013
Prerequisite An introductory writing course or equivalent
Credit Value 4 undergraduate quarter credits
Tuition $344
Description Uses descriptions of painting, film, music, architecture, and other types of art as the basis for analysis. Major emphasis is on how descriptions and organization of content serve as the basis for more complicated writing.

Writing for the Humanities, COMP 3012
Prerequisite An introductory writing course or equivalent
Credit Value 4 undergraduate quarter credits
Tuition $344
Description Emphasizes writing about the kind of texts encountered in philosophy, history, cultural anthropology, social work, and interdisciplinary fields.

Writing in the Social Sciences, COMP 3014
Prerequisite An introductory writing course or equivalent
Credit Value 4 undergraduate quarter credits
Tuition $344
Description Discusses strategies for expressing quantitative or statistical information in clear prose. Explains how statistical tables and summaries interact with written text, and how to develop narrative and descriptive techniques for producing case studies and histories.

UNIVERSITY OF MISSOURI

Center for Independent Study
136 Clark Hall
Columbia, MO 65211
Telephone: (314) 882-9596 or (800) 609-3727
Fax: (314) 882-6808
Web Site: http://indepstudy.ext.missouri.edu/
E-mail: independ@ext.missouri.edu

Accreditation   North Central Association of Colleges and Schools
Hardware Requirements   Any personal computer with a modem
Software Requirements   Most popular communications software will work
Remarks   The courses listed below are available through e-mail communication with one of the center's computers. Lessons are submitted directly to one of the computers, which scores them and generates a report containing your score, general comments on your performance, and feedback on all incorrect answers.

ACCOUNTING

Accounting I, 36
Prerequisite   Sophomore standing
Credit Value   3 undergraduate credits
Tuition $333
Description   An introductory course, covers the fundamentals of financial accounting.

Accounting II, 37
Prerequisite   Accounting I, 36
Credit Value   3 undergraduate credits
Tuition $333
Description   Covers the fundamentals of managerial accounting and advanced accounting topics.

ANIMAL SCIENCES

Horse Production, 325
Prerequisite   Four animal sciences courses
Credit Value   3 undergraduate credits
Tuition $333
Description   Provides instruction in proper ways to breed, feed, and manage horses.

ANTHROPOLOGY

General Anthropology, 1
Prerequisite   None
Credit Value   3 undergraduate credits
Tuition $333
Description   Surveys fields of anthropological concern: archaeology, cultural anthropology, physical anthropology, and linguistics. Emphasizes underlying concepts and principles in these fields.

University of Missouri
Center for Independent Study

General Information
University Courses
High School Courses
Continuing Education Courses

General Information / University Courses / High School Courses / Continuing Education Courses

Some other sites of interest:
University of Missouri Showme Home Page
University of Missouri School of Journalism Home Page
University of Missouri Extension
Edupage
Harvard Graduate School of Education
U.S. Department of Education On-Line Resources

You may contact the University of Missouri Center for Independent Study by:

- e-mail: independ@ext.missouri.edu
- telephone: 573-882-2491 or 1-800-609-3727
- fax: 573-882-6808
- postal address: 136 Clark Hall — Columbia, MO 65211

Introduction to Folklore, 184
Prerequisite None
Credit Value 3 undergraduate credits
Tuition $333
Description Introduces the study of folklore, including the mythology, approaches, and genres of folklore.

BIOLOGICAL SCIENCES

General Genetics, 202
Prerequisite Two biology and chemistry courses

Credit Value   4 undergraduate credits
Tuition $444
Description   Studies the principles of heredity and reasons for variation in plants and animals. A study of Mendelian principles and population genetics with emphasis on the human is included.

BOTANY/PLANT SCIENCE

Basic Home Horticulture, 25
Prerequisite   None
Credit Value   3 undergraduate credits
Tuition $333
Description   Includes discussions and scientific rationale of the current cultural practices for growing home horticulture plants.

Plant Propagation, 233
Prerequisite   None
Credit Value   3 undergraduate credits
Tuition $333
Description   Covers the principles and practices of the propagation of horticultural plants.

Theory and Concepts of Plant Pathology, 305
Prerequisite   Five hours of biology and junior, senior, or graduate standing
Credit value   3 undergraduate credits
Tuition $333
Description   Investigates the diseases of plants. Topics include viruses, prokaryotes, fungi, gene regulation, plant metabolism, and the genetics of plant disease.

BUSINESS

Introduction to Business Law, 254
Prerequisite   Junior standing
Credit Value   3 undergraduate credits
Tuition $333
Description   Introduces the legal aspects of business related to society—the legal system; constitutional, criminal, and tort law; contracts and sales law cases and problems; and administrative regulation of business and consumer issues.

CLASSICAL STUDIES

Classical Mythology, 60
Prerequisite   None

Credit Value   3 undergraduate credits

Tuition $333

Description   Examines how myths of Greece and Rome aid in the interpretation of literature and art.

COMMUNICATIONS

Introduction to Mass Media, 50

Prerequisite   None

Credit Value   3 undergraduate credits

Tuition $333

Description   Introduces the oral, print, and electronic media of communication. Emphasis is on history, theory, and criticism of the mass media as cultural institutions.

CRIMINOLOGY/CRIMINAL JUSTICE

Corrections, 260

Prerequisite   Introduction to Criminology and Criminal Justice, 010

Credit Value   3 undergraduate credits

Tuition $333

Description   Studies the correctional setting as an aspect of the criminal justice system, analyzing the administrative involvement, and studies the modes of organization and management that seem applicable to this type of setting.

Introduction to Criminology and Criminal Justice, 010

Prerequisite   None

Credit Value   3 undergraduate credits

Tuition $333

Description   Surveys the historical development and current status of U.S. criminal justice, including the processes, institutions, and significant problems.

Rights of the Offender, 345

Prerequisite   Previous criminal justice courses or instructor's consent

Credit Value   3 undergraduate credits

Tuition $333

Description   Addresses the constitutional protection of the accused, including an analysis of the rights guaranteed under the Fourth, Fifth, Sixth, and Fourteenth Amendments.

ECONOMICS

Introduction to the American Economy, 40

Prerequisite   None

Credit Value   3 undergraduate credits
Tuition $333
Description   An introduction to economic analysis, examines the development and operation of the U.S. economy and its evolution, institutions, and principal problems.

Introduction to Economics II, 202
Prerequisite   None
Credit Value   3 undergraduate credits
Tuition $333
Description   Focuses on microeconomics, firm analysis, the principles of supply and demand, elasticity, price determination, income distribution, and other related social and economic issues.

Money and Banking, 229
Prerequisite   Two introductory economics courses
Credit Value   3 undergraduate credits
Tuition $333
Description   Discusses the U.S. monetary and banking systems and their influence on economic activities.

Principles of Macroeconomics, 1
Prerequisite   A college algebra course
Credit Value   3 undergraduate credits
Tuition $333
Description   Surveys macroeconomic principles and their application to contemporary economic issues.

EDUCATION

The Secondary School Curriculum, T445
Prerequisite   None
Credit Value   3 undergraduate credits
Tuition $333
Description   For secondary school principals, teachers, and superintendents, presents trends in curricular change and methods of curricular investigation.

ENTOMOLOGY

Insects in the Environment, 110
Prerequisite   None
Credit Value   3 undergraduate credits
Tuition $333
Description   Introduces the study of insects, with emphasis on those species important to humans and on the general principles of integrated insect control.

EXTENSION AND ADULT EDUCATION

Extension Organization and Administration, 405
Prerequisite   None
Credit Value   3 undergraduate credits
Tuition $333
Description   Studies the principles of administration and organization and their application to extension work.

Fundamentals of Extension Teaching of Adults, 406
Prerequisite   Instructor's consent
Credit Value   3 undergraduate credits
Tuition $333
Description   Examines the special needs of adult students in extension education, including a study of classroom techniques.

Program Development and Evaluation, 403
Prerequisite   None
Credit Value   3 undergraduate credits
Tuition $333
Description   Examines the principles and procedures of program development and evaluation used in extension and other adult education agencies. Includes a review of concepts found useful in curriculum development.

FINANCE, PERSONAL

Principles of Finance, 123
Prerequisite   None
Credit Value   3 undergraduate credits
Tuition $333
Description   Topics include budgeting taxes, housing and auto loans, credit, insurance, mutual funds, stocks, bonds, and retirement planning.

GEOGRAPHY

Geography of Missouri, 225
Prerequisite   Regions and Nations of the World I or junior standing
Credit Value   3 undergraduate credits
Tuition $333
Description   Topics include the physical, human, economic, and political geography of Missouri. Also studies how geography applies to current state issues.

Physical Geography, 111
Prerequisite Regions and Nations of the World I or II or sophomore standing
Credit Value 3 undergraduate credits
Tuition $333
Description An introductory study of the physical environment: maps, landforms, water, elements of climate, climatic types, soils, and vegetation.

Regions and Nations of the World I, 1
Prerequisite None
Credit Value 3 undergraduate credits
Tuition $333
Description An introductory course that studies regional character: spatial relationships, and major problems of Europe, the United States and Canada, and Latin America, organized around geographic concepts.

Regions and Nations of the World II, 2
Prerequisite None
Credit Value 3 undergraduate credits
Tuition $333
Description Similar to Regions and Nations of the World I, except focuses on the major problems of the Commonwealth of Independent States, the Middle East, the Orient, Africa, and the Pacific world.

GEOLOGY

Earth Science, 56
Prerequisite None
Credit Value 3 undergraduate credits
Tuition $333
Description Designed for nongeology majors, provides a general study of the earth: its origins, the development of its crustal features and the processes that shape them, its oceans, its climates, and its neighbors in the solar system.

Physical Geology, 51
Prerequisite None
Credit Value 4 undergraduate credits
Tuition $444
Description Studies the materials of the earth's crust, structure and geologic features of the earth's surface, common minerals and rocks, and topographic and geologic maps.

HISTORY

Britain, 1688 to the Present, 106
Prerequisite None
Credit Value 3 undergraduate credits
Tuition $333
Description Surveys modern Britain from the era of the Restoration and Glorious Revolution (1660–1689) to the present. Major themes include the social, intellectual, cultural, political, and economic aspects of modern and contemporary Britain.

History of Missouri, 210
Prerequisite None
Credit Value 3 undergraduate credits
Tuition $333
Description Surveys Missouri political, social, economic, and cultural development, from the beginning of settlement to the present.

History of the Old South, 359
Prerequisite None
Credit Value 3 undergraduate credits
Tuition $333
Description Studies the history of the American South from colonial times to the start of the Civil War.

Survey of American History since 1865, 4
Prerequisite None
Credit Value 4 undergraduate credits
Tuition $444
Description An introduction to U.S. history since the end of the Civil War. Surveys political, economic, social, and cultural development of the American people.

Western Civilization since 1600, 202
Prerequisite None
Credit Value 3 undergraduate credits
Tuition $333
Description Studies modern Western civilization from the seventeenth century to the present, with special emphasis on the philosophical, political, social, and economic backgrounds of modern society.

JOURNALISM

High School Journalism, 380
Prerequisite   None
Credit Value   2 undergraduate credits
Tuition $222
Description   Provides a basic background in journalism and guidelines on how to teach it at the secondary level. An analysis of problems facing scholastic journalism is included.

History of American Journalism, 309
Prerequisite   None
Credit Value   3 undergraduate credits
Tuition $333
Description   Examines the U.S. mass media from colonial days to the present in the context of social, economic, and political change.

LITERATURE

Gothic Fiction, 101
Prerequisite   None
Credit Value   3 undergraduate credits
Tuition $333
Description   A survey of English and American gothic fiction from the eighteenth century to the present, examining major novels and short stories that define the gothic tradition. Includes works by Shelley, Stoker, Stevenson, Walpole, and Radcliffe.

Literature of the New Testament, 124
Prerequisite   None
Credit Value   3 undergraduate credits
Tuition $333
Description   Presents a comprehensive understanding of the New Testament: its literary background and its significance for Western civilization.

Literature of the Old Testament, 125
Prerequisite   Instructor's consent or sophomore standing
Credit Value   3 undergraduate credits
Tuition $333
Description   Analyzes representative stories, themes, and concepts of the Old Testament by examining nineteen of its books from a literary perspective.

Literary Types, 12
Prerequisite   None
Credit Value   3 undergraduate credits
Tuition $333
Description   Introduces the student to various literary types, including poetry, drama, and the short story.

Major Authors (Shakespeare), 135
Prerequisite   A course on exposition and argumentation
Credit Value   3 undergraduate credits
Tuition $333
Description   Studies Shakespeare's life and includes reading of thirteen of his major plays—histories, comedies, and tragedies—that represent all phases of his development.

MANAGEMENT

Fundamentals of Management, 202
Prerequisite   Junior standing
Credit Value   3 undergraduate credits
Tuition $333
Description   An organizational course that introduces the basic concepts of management and their application to operations and human resource management.

Human Resource Management, 310
Prerequisite   Fundamentals of Management, 202, or instructor's consent
Credit Value   3 undergraduate credits
Tuition $333
Description   Includes workforce policies and procedures of the business enterprise.

Organizational Theory, 330
Prerequisite   Fundamentals of Management, 202, or instructor's consent
Credit Value   3 undergraduate credits
Tuition $333
Description   Examines what an organization is and how it functions. Topics include theories and practical information about organizations, models for decision-making, and environmental factors and their effects on organizations.

MARKETING

Fundamentals of Marketing, 204
Prerequisite   Junior standing

Credit Value   3 undergraduate credits
Tuition $333
Description   Studies institutions, processes, and problems involved in transferring goods from producer to consumer. Emphasis is on the economic and social aspects of the transfer.

PHILOSOPHY

Ethics and the Professions, 135
Prerequisite   Sophomore standing
Credit Value   3 undergraduate credits
Tuition $333
Description   Examines ethical issues confronted by individuals in professions such as medicine, law, business, journalism, and engineering.

General Introduction to Philosophy, 1
Prerequisite   None
Credit Value   3 undergraduate credits
Tuition $333
Description   An introduction to traditional philosophical problems and methods of philosophical inquiry. Consideration is given to different philosophical theories on reality, humanity, nature, and God.

Introduction to Logic, 52
Prerequisite   None
Credit Value   3 undergraduate credits
Tuition $333
Description   Studies the basic rules of informal and of symbolic logic, including discussions on the types of argumentation, methods of reasoning, valid reasoning, and inductive and deductive reasoning.

PHYSICAL EDUCATION/HEALTH

The American Health Care System, 210HM
Prerequisite   None
Credit Value   3 undergraduate credits
Tuition $333
Description   Provides a basic understanding of the major components of the U.S. health care system: financing, planning, and regulating. Emphasis is on current issues and their impact on the delivery system.

Elements of Health Education, H65
Prerequisite   None
Credit Value   2 undergraduate credits
Tuition $222

Description   Investigates the health needs of university students and school-aged children through an examination of personal and community health problems.

Topics in Health Services Management, 201
Prerequisite   None
Credit Value   3 undergraduate credits
Tuition $333
Description   Presents the basic theories, concepts, and tools of economics that can be used to evaluate systematically the characteristics of an individual, organization, or industry.

POLITICAL SCIENCE

International Relations, 55
Prerequisite   None
Credit Value   3 undergraduate credits
Tuition $333
Description   Provides theories and analyses on various international topics, including three schools of thought in the area of international relations: idealism, realism, and transnationalism.

Introduction to Political Science, 11
Prerequisite   None
Credit Value   3 undergraduate credits
Tuition $333
Description   Discusses the scope and content of politics, and studies the theory and operation of democratic and nondemocratic governments.

Introduction to Public Administration, 310
Prerequisite   None
Credit Value   3 undergraduate credits
Tuition $333
Description   Surveys recurring themes, conceptual problems, and substantive findings in public administration literature, with particular attention to U.S. public bureaucracies.

The Politics of the Third World, 350
Prerequisite   None
Credit Value   3 undergraduate credits
Tuition $333
Description   Explores the processes and problems of the developing nations of the world. Also examines the internal political processes of third world nations, as well as the position of the third world in international affairs.

State Government, 102
Prerequisite   None
Credit Value   3 undergraduate credits
Tuition $333
Description   Studies government and politics at the state level, with emphasis on the state of Missouri.

U.S. Defense Policy Making, 335
Prerequisite   None
Credit Value   3 undergraduate credits
Tuition $333
Description   Follows the evolution of U.S. defense policy-making since World War II. Special emphasis is given to strategic policies and weapons systems and to the political processes through which these are selected and implemented.

PSYCHOLOGY

Adolescent Development, A208
Prerequisite   A general psychology course
Credit Value   2 undergraduate credits
Tuition $222
Description   Studies the psychological, intellectual, social, and physical development of adolescents.

Adolescent Psychology, 271
Prerequisite   A general psychology course
Credit Value   3 undergraduate credits
Tuition $333
Description   Studies the principles of biological, behavioral, and personality development, from puberty to maturity.

Animal Behavior, 330
Prerequisite   A general psychology course plus eight hours of psychology or biological sciences
Credit Value   3 undergraduate credits
Tuition $333
Description   Presents a comparative study of animal behavior, and teaches how behavior relates to bodily structure and environment.

Child Development, A207
Prerequisite   A general psychology course
Credit Value   2 undergraduate credits
Tuition $222

Description Studies the psychological, intellectual, social, and physical development of children.

Child Psychology, 170
Prerequisite A general psychology course
Credit Value 3 undergraduate credits
Tuition $333
Description Introduces the scientific study of the physical, cognitive, and psychosocial development of the child, from point of conception until adolescence.

Cognitive Psychology, 494
Prerequisite Varies from nine hours of psychology to graduate standing
Credit Value 3 undergraduate credits
Tuition $333
Description Focuses on basic research on human perception, memory, attention, and thought.

Educational Measurement, A280
Prerequisite A general psychology course
Credit Value 2 undergraduate credits
Tuition $222
Description Studies the basic concepts of standardized testing, evaluation techniques, and interpretation of test scores, and addresses ways that these concepts can improve the instructional process.

Environmental Psychology, 315
Prerequisite A general psychology course
Credit Value 3 undergraduate credits
Tuition $333
Description Studies the psychological effects of various environmental and socially relevant problems. Topics include environmental perception, attitudes toward the environment, and the effects of urban environments.

Foundations of Educational and Psychological Measurement, A380
Prerequisite A general psychology course or a beginning statistics course
Credit Value 3 undergraduate credits
Tuition $333
Description Addresses basic principles of educational and psychological measurement, which include test construction, validity, reliability, item analysis, and derived scores.

General Psychology, 1
Prerequisite None

Credit Value   3 undergraduate credits
Tuition $333
Description   Provides a historical background of the psychology and principles of human behavior. Includes an introduction to human growth and development, intelligence, motivation, emotions, and personality development.

Human Learning, 212
Prerequisite   A general psychology course
Credit Value   3 undergraduate credits
Tuition $333
Description   Studies the principles of learning and forgetting and the factors that affect human learning and retention.

Industrial Psychology, 212R
Prerequisite   A general psychology course
Credit Value   3 undergraduate credits
Tuition $333
Description   Examines the principles involved as employees interact with the social and physical events in their industrial work environment.

Learning and Instruction, A205
Prerequisite   A general psychology course
Credit Value   2 undergraduate credits
Tuition $222
Description   Examines the nature of human learning processes and includes implications for instruction. Emphasis is on the bases of learning, readiness for learning, types of learning, and memory.

Perception, 393
Prerequisite   Six hours of psychology
Credit Value   3 undergraduate credits
Tuition $333
Description   Studies the general characteristics of the senses and the basic conditions and principles of human perception, with emphasis on auditory and visual perception.

SOCIAL WORK

Policy and Service Delivery in Social Work, 403
Prerequisite   None
Credit Value   3 graduate credits
Tuition $421.50
Description   Based on the concepts of human need and social justice, this

course provides a historical and analytical approach to social welfare policies and programs.

Social Justice and Social Policy, 303
Prerequisite   Social Welfare and Social Work, 125
Credit Value   3 undergraduate credits
Tuition $333
Description   Based on the concepts of human need and social justice, provides a historical and analytical approach to social welfare policies and programs.

Social Welfare and Social Work, 125
Prerequisite   None
Credit Value   3 undergraduate credits
Tuition $333
Description   Examines the nature of social welfare institutions and social work and the relationship between them. Focuses on policy issues, with special reference to poverty, racism, and sexism.

SOCIOLOGY

Criminology, 211
Prerequisite   None
Credit Value   3 undergraduate credits
Tuition $333
Description   Topics include the sociology of law, the constitutional, psychological, and sociological theories of criminal behavior, the process of criminal justice, the treatment of corrections, and the control of crime.

Rural Sociology, 1
Prerequisite   None
Credit Value   3 undergraduate credits
Tuition $333
Description   Introduces students to the sociology of rural and small towns, including the structure, functioning, and trends of rural society.

Urban Sociology, 216
Prerequisite   Rural Sociology, 1, or an introductory sociology course
Credit Value   3 undergraduate credits
Tuition $333
Description   Studies urbanism as a world phenomenon, including the ecological and demographic characteristics of cities and the organization of urban society.

SPECIAL EDUCATION

Introduction to Mental Retardation, 313
Prerequisite   Introduction to Special Education, L311
Credit Value   3 undergraduate credits
Tuition $333
Description   An introductory course that describes the characteristics, classification, and causes of mental retardation and severe handicaps.

Introduction to Special Education, L311
Prerequisite   None
Credit Value   3 undergraduate credits
Tuition $333
Description   A study of special children and youth: their characteristics, prevalence, and etiological background.

UNIVERSITY OF NORTHERN COLORADO

College of Continuing Education
501 20th Street
Greeley, CO 80639
Telephone: (303) 351-2331
Fax: (303) 351-1837
E-mail: micadams@blue.univnorthco.edu

Accreditation   North Central Association of Colleges and Schools
Hardware Requirements   Most personal computers with a modem will work
Software Requirements   Most popular communications software and access providers will work
Remarks   The university currently offers only one noncredit course that can be taken from your home or office computer.

COMMUNICATIONS

Speeding along the Internet, INT 000
Prerequisite   None
Credit Value   Noncredit, but a 2-credit option is in development
Tuition $159
Description   Conducted through electronic mail, this course provides a comprehensive and working knowledge of the Internet.

UNIVERSITY OF TEXAS AT AUSTIN

Distance Education Center
P.O. Box 7700
Austin, TX 78713-7700
Telephone: (512) 471-7716 or (800) 252-3461
Fax: (512) 471-7853
Web Site: http://www.utexas.edu/depts/eimc/
E-mail: dec@www.utexas.edu

Accreditation   Southern Association of Colleges and Schools
Hardware Requirements   Any personal computer with communications capability
Software Requirements   Most popular communications software will work
Remarks   The university currently offers the following courses through an electronic mail option but is currently developing a more interactive computer conferencing approach to these and additional courses.

ANTHROPOLOGY

Human Origins and Evolution, ANT 348
Prerequisite   None
Credit Value   3 undergraduate credits
Tuition $170
Description   A detailed examination and analysis of morphological trends evident in the hominid fossil record.

Physical Anthropology, ANT 301
Prerequisite   None
Credit Value   3 undergraduate credits
Tuition $170
Description   Covers human evolution, race, heredity, the organic basis of culture, and culture history through the Paleolithic stage.

HISTORY

English Civilization before 1603, HIS 304K
Prerequisite   None
Credit Value   3 undergraduate credits
Tuition $170
Description   Covers prehistoric and Roman Britain through the introduction of Christianity, the Reformation, and the reign of Elizabeth I.

English Civilization since 1603, HIS 304L
Prerequisite   None

Credit Value   3 undergraduate credits
Tuition $170
Description   Covers the British Civil War, the Restoration, the American Revolution, the British Empire, and the two world wars.

Texas and Its History, HIS 366N
Prerequisite   Upper division standing
Credit Value   3 undergraduate credits
Tuition $170
Description   Examines the development of Texas from the period before the arrival of Europeans through the modern era with its urbanization.

The United States, 1492–1865, HIS 315K
Prerequisite   None
Credit Value   3 undergraduate credits
Tuition $170
Description   Covers from the discoveries through the end of the Civil War.

The United States since 1865, HIS 315L
Prerequisite   None
Credit Value   3 undergraduate credits
Tuition $170
Description   Covers U.S. history and development since the end of the Civil War.

Western Civilization in Medieval Times, HIS 309K
Prerequisite   None
Credit Value   3 undergraduate credits
Tuition $170
Description   Covers the growth of European civilization from prehistory to the end of the seventeenth century.

Western Civilization in Modern Times, HIS 309L
Prerequisite   None
Credit Value   3 undergraduate credits
Tuition $170
Description   A study of European civilization from 1700 to the present.

LITERATURE

American Literature: From the Beginnings to 1865, E 337
Prerequisite   None
Credit Value   3 undergraduate credits
Tuition $170
Description   A survey of major writers of poetry and prose.

American Literature: From 1865 to the Present, E 338
Prerequisite   None
Credit Value   3 undergraduate credits
Tuition $170
Description   A survey of major writers of poetry and prose.

American Science Fiction, E 376L
Prerequisite   None
Credit Value   3 undergraduate credits
Tuition $175
Description   Covers the development of American science fiction from the 1920s to the 1980s. Basic course structure follows the historical development of the genre.

Masterworks of Literature: American, E 316K
Prerequisite   Completion of at least 27 hours of course work, including a course in rhetoric and composition
Credit Value   3 undergraduate credits
Tuition $170
Description   An introduction to masterpieces of the literary tradition, emphasizing historical, generic, and thematic connections and including major American writers in poetry, prose, and drama.

Shakespeare: Selected Plays, E 321
Prerequisite   None
Credit Value   3 undergraduate credits
Tuition $185
Description   Provides a representative selection of Shakespeare's best comedies, tragedies, and histories.

WRITING

Topics in Writing, E 309K
Prerequisite   None
Credit Value   3 undergraduate credits
Tuition $170
Description   Examines literature and composition.

UNIVERSITY OF WASHINGTON EXTENSION

Distance Learning, Campus Box 354223
5001 25th Avenue, NE
Seattle, WA 98105-4190

Telephone: (206) 543-2350 or (800) 543-2320
Fax: (206) 685-9359
Web Site: http://weber.u.washington.edu/~instudy/
E-mail: instudy@u.washington.edu

Accreditation   Northwest Association of Schools and Colleges
Hardware Requirements   Any personal computer with communications capability
Software Requirements   Most popular communications software will work
Remarks   The university offers an extensive array of correspondence-based courses for those interested.

ACCOUNTING

Fundamentals of Managerial Accounting, ACCTG C230
Prerequisite   A course in the fundamentals of financial accounting
Credit Value   3 undergraduate quarter credits
Tuition $210
Description   An analysis and evaluation of accounting information as part of the managerial processes of planning, decision-making, and control.

ARCHITECTURE

Romanesque, Gothic and Renaissance Architecture, ARCH C351
Prerequisite   None
Credit Value   3 undergraduate quarter credits
Tuition $210
Description   Explores architectural history in the Western world from A.D. 550 to 1750.

ASTRONOMY

Astronomy, ASTR C101
Prerequisite   None
Credit Value   5 undergraduate quarter credits
Tuition $350
Description   An introduction to the universe with emphasis on conceptual, as contrasted with mathematical, comprehension.

The Planets, ASTR C150
Prerequisite   None
Credit Value   5 undergraduate quarter credits
Tuition $350

Description A survey of the planets of the solar system, with emphasis on recent space exploration of the planets and on the comparative evolution of Earth and the other planets.

ATMOSPHERIC SCIENCE

Weather, ATMS C101
Prerequisite None
Credit Value 5 undergraduate quarter credits
Tuition $350
Description Discusses Earth's atmosphere, with emphasis on weather observations and forecasting. Includes daily weather map discussions and physical processes involved in weather phenomena.

CHEMISTRY

General Chemistry 140, CHEM C140
Prerequisite High school chemistry and/or physics
Credit Value 4 undergraduate quarter credits
Tuition $280
Description Topics include atomic nature of matter, nuclear chemistry, stoichiometry, the periodic table, quantum concepts, chemical bonding, and gas laws.

General Chemistry 150, CHEM C150
Prerequisite CHEM C140
Credit Value 4 undergraduate quarter credits
Tuition $280
Description An introduction to inorganic chemistry, solids, solutions, and acid–base chemical equilibrium.

Introduction to General Chemistry, CHEM C120
Prerequisite High school algebra or equivalent
Credit Value 5 undergraduate quarter credits
Tuition $350
Description An introduction to chemistry with at-home laboratory experiments for those with little or no chemistry background.

COMMUNICATIONS

History and Development of Communications & Journalism, CMU C201
Prerequisite None
Credit Value 5 undergraduate quarter credits
Tuition $350

Description   Covers, from prehistoric times, social and technical inventions and political and economic contexts.

Legal Aspects of Communications, CMU C320
Prerequisite   None
Credit Value   5 undergraduate quarter credits
Tuition $350
Description   Explores the regulations governing publication and broadcast in the mass media, focusing on the limits of free speech.

The Phenomena of Communicating, CMU C202
Prerequisite   None
Credit Value   5 undergraduate quarter credits
Tuition $350
Description   Explores types of communicating behavior in progressively more complex situations, from individual cognition through interpersonal interactions to mass communicating.

COMPUTER SCIENCE

C Programming: Introduction and Intermediate, C PROG C231
Prerequisite   Knowledge of one high-level programming language such as BASIC, Pascal, COBOL, or FORTRAN.
Credit Value   Noncredit
Tuition $304
Description   Covers program design and organization in C.

Developing a C Application, C PROG C900
Prerequisite   A sequence of four C programming courses or equivalent work experience
Credit Value   Noncredit
Tuition $264
Description   Designed for those with extensive knowledge and/or experience in C or C+, students develop a proposal for an application project, write a schedule, and develop the project.

ECONOMICS

Intermediate Microeconomics, ECON C300
Prerequisite   Introduction to Microeconomics, ECON C201
Credit Value   5 undergraduate quarter credits
Tuition $350
Description   Explores choice decisions of individuals and firms and the consequences of those decisions in product and factor markets.

Introduction to Macroeconomics, ECON C201
Prerequisite None
Credit Value 5 undergraduate quarter credits
Tuition $350
Description An analysis of the aggregate economy: national income, inflation, business fluctuations, and the monetary system.

Introduction to Microeconomics, ECON C200
Prerequisite None
Credit Value 5 undergraduate quarter credits
Tuition $350
Description An introduction to analysis of markets: consumer demand, production, exchange, the price system, and resource allocation.

EDUCATION

Adaptive Computer Technology, REHAB C496
Prerequisite None
Credit Value 3 undergraduate quarter credits
Tuition $210
Description Surveys the field of adaptive computer technology as it impacts the lives of people with disabilities, including the performance of tasks related to employment, education, and recreation.

Science Education: Elementary School Programs and Practices, EDC&I C470
Prerequisite Teaching experience
Credit Value 3 undergraduate quarter credits
Tuition $210
Description Designed for classroom teachers, this course emphasizes objectives, methods, and materials related to the concepts of processes of science.

Using the Internet for Curriculum Development, EDC&I C494
Prerequisite None
Credit Value 5 undergraduate quarter credits
Tuition $350
Description In this course, educators develop curriculum using the Internet as an investigational tool for classroom projects.

ENVIRONMENTAL STUDIES

Introduction to Environmental Studies, ENV S C101
Prerequisite None
Credit Value 5 undergraduate quarter credits
Tuition $350

Description   Topics include natural history and human modifications of the natural world. Evolutionary biology, physical geography, toxicology, energy, economics, law, and public policy.

GEOGRAPHY

Geography of Cities, GEOG C277
Prerequisite   None
Credit Value   5 undergraduate quarter credits
Tuition $350
Description   A study of systems of cities—their location, distribution, functions, and competition—and their internal structure.

World Regions, GEOG C102
Prerequisite   None
Credit Value   5 undergraduate quarter credits
Tuition $350
Description   Provides a spatial study of world regions based on historical, cultural, political, economic, and other factors.

GEOLOGY

Introduction to Geological Sciences, GEOL C101
Prerequisite   None
Credit Value   5 undergraduate quarter credits
Tuition $350
Description   A survey of the physical systems that give Earth its form. Emphasizes the dynamic nature of interior and surface processes and their relevance to humankind, and stresses the value of rocks and earth forms in understanding the past.

GERONTOLOGY

Biological Aspects of Aging, UCONJ C440
Prerequisite   An introductory biology course or instructor's consent
Credit Value   3 undergraduate quarter credits
Tuition $210
Description   An introductory course on aspects of the biology of human aging and of functional changes associated with normal aging and with those illnesses that may be present in the elderly.

Social and Cultural Aspects of Aging, UCONJ C442
Prerequisite   Upper division undergraduate or graduate standing
Credit Value   3 undergraduate quarter credits
Tuition $210

Description   Examines the range and variation of relationships among age-linked attitudes and cultural values related to aging.

HISTORY

History of Modern Japan, HSTAS C423
Prerequisite   None
Credit Value   5 undergraduate quarter credits
Tuition $350
Description   Surveys the political, social, economic, and cultural development of Japan from the late Tokugawa period to the present, with special emphasis on the cultural impact of the West.

A History of the United States since 1940, HSTAA C135
Prerequisite   None
Credit Value   5 undergraduate quarter credits
Tuition $350
Description   Through study of documents, personal testimony, other source materials, and written reports on historical problems, students are encouraged to examine evidence and to think "historically" about persons, events, and movements within the memory of their own generation.

The Question of Human Nature, CHID C110
Prerequisite   None
Credit Value   5 undergraduate quarter credits
Tuition $350
Description   Considers the relationship between individuals and their culture by tracing the evolution of the notion of human nature in both Europe and the United States.

Survey of the History of the United States, HSTAA C201
Prerequisite   None
Credit Value   5 undergraduate quarter credits
Tuition $350
Description   Supplies the knowledge of U.S. history that any intelligent and educated U.S. citizen should have.

LANGUAGES

Elementary Italian I, ITAL C101
Prerequisite   None
Credit Value   5 undergraduate quarter credits
Tuition $350
Description   Covers basic Italian grammar and idiomatic usage of the language. While all assignments are written, oral practice is provided by use of required tape recordings.

Elementary Italian II, ITAL C102
Prerequisite   Elementary Italian I, ITAL C101
Credit Value   5 undergraduate quarter credits
Tuition $350
Description   Continues from ITAL C101.

Elementary Italian III, ITAL C103
Prerequisite   Elementary Italian II, ITAL C102
Credit Value   5 undergraduate quarter credits
Tuition $350
Description   Continues from ITAL C102.

Elementary Spanish I, SPAN C101
Prerequisite   None
Credit Value   5 undergraduate quarter credits
Tuition $350
Description   Recommended for those who wish to work primarily toward a reading knowledge of the language. Audio tapes support the learning.

Elementary Spanish II, SPAN C102
Prerequisite   Elementary Spanish I, SPAN C101
Credit Value   5 undergraduate quarter credits
Tuition $350
Description   Continues from SPAN C101.

Elementary Spanish III, SPAN C103
Prerequisite   Elementary Spanish II, C102
Credit Value   5 undergraduate quarter credits
Tuition $350
Description   Continues from SPAN C102.

First-Year German I, GERMAN C101
Prerequisite   None
Credit Value   5 undergraduate quarter credits
Tuition $350
Description   Focuses on acquisition of a fairly large vocabulary, grammar, and practice in reading and writing.

First-Year German II, GERMAN C102
Prerequisite   First-Year German I, C101
Credit Value   5 undergraduate quarter credits
Tuition $350
Description   Continues from C101.

First-Year German III, GERMAN C103
Prerequisite   First–Year German II, C102
Credit Value   5 undergraduate quarter credits
Tuition $350
Description   Continues from C102.

LINGUISTICS

Introduction to Grammar, LING C100
Prerequisite   None
Credit Value   5 undergraduate quarter credits
Tuition $350
Description   Designed for students planning to major in foreign languages or linguistics, this course serves as an introduction to basic grammatical concepts and terminology.

Introduction to Linguistic Thought, LING C200
Prerequisite   None
Credit Value   5 undergraduate quarter credits
Tuition $350
Description   An introduction to the scientific study of language, language and writing, phonological and grammatical analysis, and related disciplines.

LITERATURE

American Literature: Contemporary America, ENGL C355
Prerequisite   None
Credit Value   5 undergraduate quarter credits
Tuition $350
Description   Focuses on the works of such writers as Ellison, Williams, O'Connor, Lowell, Barth, Rich, and Hawkes.

American Literature: The Early Modern Period, ENGL C354
Prerequisite   None
Credit Value   5 undergraduate quarter credits
Tuition $350
Description   Focuses on the works of such writers as O'Neil, Frost, Cather, Pound, Eliot, and Faulkner.

American Literature: The Early Nation, ENGL C352
Prerequisite   None
Credit Value   5 undergraduate quarter credits
Tuition $350
Description   Focuses on the works of such writers as Melville, Cooper, Poe, Hawthorne, Emerson, Dickinson, and Douglass.

The Bible as Literature, ENGL C310
Prerequisite   None
Credit Value   5 undergraduate quarter credits
Tuition $350
Description   An introduction to the development of the religious ideas and institutions of ancient Israel, with selected readings from the Old and New Testaments.

English Literature: The Late Renaissance, ENGL C325
Prerequisite   None
Credit Value   5 undergraduate quarter credits
Tuition $350
Description   Reviews a period of skepticism for some, faith for others, but intellectual upheaval generally. Includes poems by John Donne and the "metaphysical" school and poems and plays by Ben Johnson and other late rivals to Shakespeare.

Fantasy, ENGL C349
Prerequisite   None
Credit Value   5 undergraduate quarter credits
Tuition $350
Description   Surveys nonnaturalistic literature, selected folktales, fairy tales, fables, horror and ghost stories, science fiction, and/or utopian literature.

Milton, ENGL C326
Prerequisite   None
Credit Value   5 undergraduate quarter credits
Tuition $350
Description   Includes Milton's early poems and the prose—*Paradise Lost, Paradise Regained,* and *Samson Agonistes,* with attention to the religious, intellectual, and literary contexts.

The Modern Novel, ENGL C340
Prerequisite   None
Credit Value   5 undergraduate quarter credits
Tuition $350
Description   Discusses the novel on both sides of the Atlantic in the first half of the twentieth century. Includes such writers as Joyce, Waugh, Lawrence, Steinbeck, Hemingway, and Faulkner.

Reading Fiction, ENGL C242
Prerequisite   None

Credit Value   5 undergraduate quarter credits
Tuition $350
Description   Discusses critical interpretation and meaning in fiction. Includes different examples of fiction representing a variety of types from the medieval to the modern period.

Reading Literature, ENGL C200
Prerequisite   None
Credit Value   5 undergraduate quarter credits
Tuition $350
Description   Provides techniques and practices in reading and enjoying literature. Examines some of the best works in English and American literature and considers such features of literary meaning as imagery, characterization, narration, and patterning in sound and sense.

Shakespeare, ENGL C225
Prerequisite   None
Credit Value   5 undergraduate quarter credits
Tuition $350
Description   A survey of Shakespeare's career as dramatist. Studies representative comedies, tragedies, romances, and history plays.

Shakespeare after 1603, ENGL C324
Prerequisite   None
Credit Value   5 undergraduate quarter credits
Tuition $350
Description   Covers Shakespeare's career as dramatist after 1603 through a study of his comedies, tragedies, and romances.

Shakespeare to 1603, ENGL C323
Prerequisite   None
Credit Value   5 undergraduate quarter credits
Tuition $350
Description   Covers Shakespeare's career as dramatist before 1603, including *Hamlet.*

MATHEMATICS

Algebra with Applications, MATH C111
Prerequisite   One and a half years of high school algebra
Credit Value   5 undergraduate quarter credits
Tuition $350
Description   Covers the use of graphs and algebraic functions as found in business and economics and algebraic and graphical manipulations to solve problems.

Applications of Calculus to Business and Economics, MATH C112
Prerequisite   Algebra with Applications, MATH C111, or equivalent
Credit Value   5 undergraduate quarter credits
Tuition $350
Description   Topics include rates of change, tangent, derivative, accumulation, area, integral in specific contexts, particularly economics.

Elementary Linear Algebra, MATH C205
Prerequisite   MATH C112
Credit Value   3 undergraduate quarter credits
Tuition $210
Description   Topics include systems of equations, vector spaces, matrices, linear transformations, and characteristic vectors.

Introduction to Differential Equations, MATH C307
Prerequisite   Previous calculus with a geometry course
Credit Value   3 undergraduate quarter credits
Tuition $210
Description   Includes Taylor series and first and second order ordinary differential equations.

Mathematics: A Practical Art, MATH C107
Prerequisite   One and a half years of high school algebra
Credit Value   5 undergraduate quarter credits
Tuition $350
Description   Covers the exponential function and how it applies to a wide variety of phenomena and elementary probability and statistics and their use in a variety of applications.

Precalculus, MATH C120
Prerequisite   Two years of high school algebra
Credit Value   5 undergraduate quarter credits
Tuition $350
Description   Topics include polynomial, rational, exponential, and trigonometric functions.

MUSIC

History of Jazz, MUSIC C331
Prerequisite   None
Credit Value   3 undergraduate quarter credits
Tuition $210
Description   A survey of the major periods and styles of jazz, from New Orleans jazz to the avant-garde and popular jazz today. Studies the main characteristics of each style.

NUTRITION

Nutrition for Today, NUTR C300
Prerequisite None
Credit Value 3 undergraduate quarter credits
Tuition $210
Description Covers basic and applied nutrition and food science. Identification and physiological roles of nutrients, nutritional requirements, problems with over- and undernutrition, and nutritional food-related diseases.

OCEANOGRAPHY

Survey of Oceanography, OCEAN C101
Prerequisite None
Credit Value 5 undergraduate quarter credits
Tuition $350
Description Includes the origin and extent of the oceans, the nature of the sea bottom, the causes and effects of currents and tides, and animal and plant life in the sea.

PHILOSOPHY

Introduction to Logic, PHIL C120
Prerequisite None
Credit Value 5 undergraduate quarter credits
Tuition $350
Description Introduces elementary symbolic logic: the development, application, and theoretical properties of an artificial symbolic language designed to provide a clear presentation of the logical structure of deductive arguments.

Philosophical Issues and the Law, PHIL C114
Prerequisite None
Credit Value 5 undergraduate quarter credits
Tuition $350
Description Analyzes and critically assesses various philosophical issues in law and legal reasoning. Topics include criminal responsibility, civil disobedience, abortion, reverse discrimination, and enforcement of morals.

Practical Reasoning, PHIL C115
Prerequisite None
Credit Value 5 undergraduate quarter credits
Tuition $350

Description   An introduction to logic, emphasizing concepts and methods used for practical analysis of arguments in everyday contexts.

PHYSICAL EDUCATION/HEALTH

Medical Aspects of Disability for Vocational Counseling, REHAB C496
Prerequisite   None
Credit Value   3 undergraduate quarter credits or 3 graduate credits
Tuition $210 for undergraduate credit, $495 for graduate credit
Description   Designed for professionals who deal with individuals with disabilities, whether as counselors, teachers, therapists, or others, this course covers the most common disabling conditions. Uses videotaped lectures as its base.

POLITICAL SCIENCE

American Foreign Policy, POL S C321
Prerequisite   Introduction to Politics, POL S C101
Credit Value   5 undergraduate quarter credits
Tuition $350
Description   Explores the constitutional framework, major factors in the formulation and execution of foreign policy, and the principal policymakers and the various groups that influence them.

Environmental Politics and Policy in the United States, POL S C383
Prerequisite   None
Credit Value   5 undergraduate quarter credits
Tuition $350
Description   Discusses interrelations between technological and environmental change and policy reform. Considers political behavior related to these phenomena and the capacity of urban public organizations to predict change and formulate new policies.

Introduction to International Relations, POL S C203
Prerequisite   None
Credit Value   5 undergraduate quarter credits
Tuition $350
Description   Analyzes the world community, its politics, and governments.

Introduction to Politics, POL S C101
Prerequisite   None
Credit Value   5 undergraduate quarter credits
Tuition $350
Description   An introduction to thinking about the political problems that affect our lives and shape the world around us.

The Politics of Mass Communication in America, POL S C305
Prerequisite   None
Credit Value   5 undergraduate quarter credits
Tuition $350
Description   Examines the role of mass audiences in politics from the standpoint of the communications strategies used to shape their political involvement. Topics include social structure and political participation, political propaganda, and persuasion.

PSYCHOLOGY

Abnormal Psychology, PSYCH C305
Prerequisite   10 credits in psychology
Credit Value   5 undergraduate quarter credits
Tuition $350
Description   An overview of major categories of psychopathology, including description and classification, theoretical models, and recent research on etiology and treatment.

Developmental Psychology, PSYCH C306
Prerequisite   Psychology as a Social Science, PSYCH C101
Credit Value   5 undergraduate quarter credits
Tuition $350
Description   An analysis of psychological development of the child in relation to biological, physical, and sociological antecedent conditions from infancy to adolescence.

Elementary Psychology, PSYCH C213
Prerequisite   Fundamentals of Psychological Research, PSYCH C209, plus one and a half years of high school algebra
Credit Value   6 undergraduate quarter credits
Tuition $420
Description   Covers applied statistics in psychology, and describes data, probability theory, and stating and testing hypotheses in psychology. Covers the more commonly used inference tests.

Fundamentals of Psychological Research, PSYCH C209
Prerequisite   Psychology as a Social Science, PSYCH C101
Credit Value   4 undergraduate quarter credits
Tuition $280
Description   Examines psychological research methodology and techniques. Topics include the logic of hypothesis testing, experimental design, research strategies and techniques, and fundamentals of scientific writing.

Introduction to Drugs and Behavior, PSYCH C322
Prerequisite None
Credit Value 3 undergraduate quarter credits
Tuition $210
Description Covers the basic concept of drug action emphasizing the behavioral consequences of the intake of a variety of drugs.

Introduction to Personality and Individual Differences, PSYCH C205
Prerequisite Psychology as a Social Science, PSYCH C101
Credit Value 4 undergraduate quarter credits
Tuition $280
Description Introduces basic concepts, methods, and background for a more intensive study in the field of personality.

Personality Development of the Child, PSYCH C415
Prerequisite Developmental Psychology, PSYCH C306
Credit Value 5 undergraduate quarter credits
Tuition $350
Description Covers socialization theory and research, infant attachment and social relationships, development of aggressive and altruistic behaviors, sex-role development, moral development, and parent and adult influences.

Psychology as a Social Science, PSYCH C101
Prerequisite None
Credit Value 5 undergraduate quarter credits
Tuition $350
Description Examines behavior from a social science viewpoint. Emphasizes personality, individual differences, attitudes, and social behavior and influence. Includes related aspects of cognition, behavior disorders, states of awareness, motivation and emotion, and learning.

Social Psychology, PSYCH C345
Prerequisite Psychology as a Social Science, PSYCH C101
Credit Value 5 undergraduate quarter credits
Tuition $350
Description Covers the effects of the social environment on the formation of individual attitudes, values, and beliefs and on individual and group behavior. Discusses major theoretical approaches of field and experimental research findings.

Survey of Cognitive Psychology, PSYCH C355
Prerequisite 8 credits in psychology, including an introductory course
Credit Value 5 undergraduate quarter credits
Tuition $350

Description Discusses current theory and research in perception, attention, memory and learning, attitudes, thinking and decision-making, and language.

RELIGION

Introduction to World Religions: Eastern Traditions, RELIG C202
Prerequisite None
Credit Value 5 undergraduate quarter credits
Tuition $350
Description An introduction to the history of religions, concentrating on religions that have developed in Southeast and East Asia, with primary attention to Hinduism and Buddhism. Other important Asian religions are discussed in relation to them, with emphasis on basic conceptual and symbolic structures.

SOCIOLOGY

Criminology, SOC C371
Prerequisite None
Credit Value 5 undergraduate quarter credits
Tuition $350
Description A survey of legal definitions, types of criminal behavior, trends and patterns, recidivism, characteristics of offenders, environmental influences, diagnostic methods, and prediction and prevention.

Socialization, SOC C347
Prerequisite None
Credit Value 5 undergraduate quarter credits
Tuition $350
Description How social systems control the behavior of their constituent groups and persons through the socialization process, sanctions, power, allocation of status, and rewards.

Survey of Sociology, SOC C110
Prerequisite None
Credit Value 5 undergraduate quarter credits
Tuition $350
Description Surveys human interaction, social institutions, social stratification, socialization, deviance, social control, and social and cultural change.

STATISTICS

Basic Statistics, STAT C220
Prerequisite One and a half years of high school algebra

Credit Value   5 undergraduate quarter credits

Tuition $350

Description   Covers the objectives and pitfalls of statistical studies. Includes the structure of data sets, histograms, and means and standard deviations; correlation and regression; and probability theory and the binomial and normal distributions.

Basic Statistics with Applications, STAT C301

Prerequisite   One and a half years of high school algebra

Credit Value   5 undergraduate quarter credits

Tuition $350

Description   Similar to Basic Statistics, STAT C220, but focuses on the application to problems in the student's major field of study.

Elements of Statistical Methods, STAT C311

Prerequisite   None

Credit Value   5 undergraduate quarter credits

Tuition $350

Description   Covers elementary concepts of probability and sampling. Includes basic concepts of hypothesis testing, estimation and confidence intervals, t-tests, and chi-square tests.

WRITING

Advanced Expository Writing, ENGL C381

Prerequisite   Sophomore standing

Credit Value   5 undergraduate quarter credits

Tuition $350

Description   Concentrates on the development of prose style for experienced writers.

Beginning Short Story Writing, ENGL C284

Prerequisite   None

Credit Value   5 undergraduate quarter credits

Tuition $350

Description   Introduces the theory and practice of writing the short story.

Composition: Exposition, ENGL C131

Prerequisite   None

Credit Value   5 undergraduate quarter credits

Tuition $350

Description   Allows students to study and practice good writing. Topics used are derived from a variety of personal, academic, and public subjects. This course can be previewed online before signing up. The course guide is available at the University of Washington web site (see earlier).

Intermediate Expository Writing, ENGL C281
Prerequisite Sophomore standing
Credit Value 5 undergraduate quarter credits
Tuition $350
Description Provides help in writing papers communicating information and opinion to develop accurate, competent, and effective expression. This course can be previewed at the University of Washington web site (see earlier).

Intermediate Seminar: Short Story Writing, ENGL C384
Prerequisite None
Credit Value 5 undergraduate quarter credits
Tuition $350
Description Explores and develops continuity in the elements of fiction writing. Includes methods of extending and sustaining plot and setting character, point of view, and tone.

Introduction to Technical Writing, ENGR C231
Prerequisite One 5-credit composition course
Credit Value 3 undergraduate quarter credits
Tuition $210
Description Includes principles of organizing, developing, and writing technical information. Covers report forms and rhetorical patterns common to scientific and technical disciplines and such technical writing conventions as headings, illustrations, style, and tone.

6 Directory of Undergraduate and Graduate Degree Programs Available Online

The degree programs included in this directory are those in which students can earn most or all required credits through online courses and projects. As additional colleges and universities learn more about the available technologies and ways in which to offer online programs, the number of such programs will rapidly increase.

This directory offers complete details on the online degree programs currently available. Both undergraduate and graduate degree programs are included, as well as several certificate programs. Certificate programs are generally taken by individuals who have already earned an undergraduate or even graduate degree in their chosen field. They usually use professional certificate programs from accredited colleges and universities to demonstrate a high level of knowledge in another, often related, field.

To help you locate the degree programs you are seeking, an easy-to-use Online Degree Program Locator is provided. Before you begin reviewing individual programs, you should read through the entire list of programs in the locator. Often, different schools describe programs on similar subjects differently, or combine subjects, so it is best to go through the complete locator. Some terms in the locator cover numerous subject areas, so be sure to review programs with broad-sounding titles.

The selection of undergraduate, graduate, and career-enhancing certificate programs in this directory should enable most readers to find the program they need. If not, you will find that many of these programs will be glad to offer alternatives or even tailor a program to your specific needs. Don't be afraid to ask if a program can be altered for your requirements. The people who run these programs have your needs in mind and will do everything possible to accommodate you in your quest for higher education.

THE EASY-TO-USE ONLINE DEGREE PROGRAM LOCATOR

The locator is arranged in alphabetical order by the subject area of each degree or certificate program. Following each alphabetical entry are the programs available online for that subject area and the institutions offering them.

Once you find a subject area or areas that interest you, simply turn to the alphabetical listing of colleges and universities following the locator for full descriptions of the programs.

Accounting
   Bachelor of Science, City University
Aeronautical Science
   Master of, Embry-Riddle Aeronautical University
Applied Arts and Sciences
   Bachelor of Science, Rochester Institute of Technology
Applied Computing and Communications
   Professional Certificate, Rochester Institute of Technology
Art Appreciation/Art History
   Bachelor of Arts, City University
Behavioral Sciences
   Bachelor of Arts, University of Maryland
   Bachelor of Science, New York Institute of Technology
   Bachelor of Science, University of Maryland
Business Administration
   Associate of Arts, Rogers State College
   Bachelor of Science, City University
   Bachelor of Science, New York Institute of Technology
   Bachelor of Science, University of Phoenix
   M.B.A., International School of Information Management
   M.B.A., University of Phoenix

Business Information Systems
  Bachelor of Science, University of Phoenix
Business Management
  Bachelor of Science, University of Phoenix
Communications Management
  Certificate, Rutgers
Computer Information Systems
  Master of Science, University of Phoenix
Computer Networking
  Bachelor of Science, City University
Computer Programming
  Associate of Applied Science, Rogers State College
  Bachelor of Science, City University
Computer Science
  Associate of Applied Science, Rogers State College
  Bachelor of Arts, University of Maryland
  Bachelor of Science, University of Maryland
Computer Studies
  Bachelor of Arts, University of Maryland
  Bachelor of Science, University of Maryland
Computer Systems
  Bachelor of Science, City University
Data Communications
  Professional Certificate, Rochester Institute of Technology
Economics
  Bachelor of Arts, City University
Electrical/Mechanical Technology
  Bachelor of Science, Rochester Institute of Technology
Emergency Management
  Professional Certificate, Rochester Institute of Technology
Energy & Environmental Quality Management
  Bachelor of Science, City University
Environmental Management
  Professional Certificate, Rochester Institute of Technology
Film History
  Bachelor of Arts, City University
Film Theory
  Bachelor of Arts, City University

Fire Science Management
   Bachelor of Arts, University of Maryland
   Bachelor of Science, University of Maryland
General Studies
   Bachelor of Science, City University
Hazardous Materials Management
   Certificate, University of California
Hazardous Materials Technology
   Certificate, Eastern Iowa Community College District
Health Systems Administration
   Master of Science, Rochester Institute of Technology
   Professional Certificate, Rochester Institute of Technology
History
   Bachelor of Arts, City University
Humanities
   Bachelor of Arts, City University
   Master of Arts, California State University, Dominguez Hills
Industrial Technology
   Master of Science, East Carolina University
Information Management
   Master of Science, International School of Information Management
Information Technology
   Master of Science, Rochester Institute of Technology
Integral Studies
   Doctor of Philosophy (Ph.D.), California Institute for Integral Studies
Interdisciplinary
   Bachelor of Arts, New York Institute of Technology
   Bachelor of Professional Studies, New York Institute of Technology
   Bachelor of Science, New York Institute of Technology
   Doctor of Philosophy (Ph.D.), The Union Institute
International Business
   International M.B.A., University of Phoenix
International Studies
   Bachelor of Arts, City University
   Master of Arts, Salve Regina University
Journalism
   Bachelor of Arts, City University
Law Enforcement Administration
   Bachelor of Science, City University

Liberal Arts
  Associate of Arts, Rogers State College
Literature
  Bachelor of Arts, City University
Management
  Bachelor of Arts, University of Maryland
  Bachelor of Science, City University
  Bachelor of Science, University of Maryland
  Master of Science, Thomas Edison State College
Management Studies
  Bachelor of Arts, University of Maryland
  Bachelor of Science, University of Maryland
Marketing
  Bachelor of Arts, City University
  Bachelor of Science, City University
Mathematics
  Bachelor of Arts, City University
Organizational Management
  Master of Arts, University of Phoenix
Paralegal Studies
  Bachelor of Arts, University of Maryland
  Bachelor of Science, University of Maryland
Philosophy
  Bachelor of Arts, City University
Political Science
  Bachelor of Arts, City University
Psychology
  Bachelor of Arts, City University
Sociology
  Bachelor of Arts, City University
Software Development & Management
  Master of Science, Rochester Institute of Technology
Technology and Management
  Bachelor of Arts, University of Maryland
  Bachelor of Science, University of Maryland
  M.B.A. in Technology Management, University of Phoenix
Telecommunications Management
  Bachelor of Science, City University
  Professional Certificate, Rochester Institute of Technology

Voice Communications
Professional Certificate, Rochester Institute of Technology

HOW TO READ THE DESCRIPTIONS

Following is an explanation of each caption used to describe the degree and certificate programs included in the directory.

Institution   The complete name and address of the college, institute, or university sponsoring the programs described.

Contact   The name, telephone number, toll-free number (if one is available), fax number, and electronic address of the individual or office to contact for additional information or details concerning registration.

Accreditation   The name of the association that has accredited the institution, as well as the association accrediting individual programs, where appropriate. Only schools accredited by an association recognized by the U.S. Department of Education and/or the Council on Recognition of Postsecondary Accreditation are included in this directory.

Degrees Offered Online   The degrees and/or certificates available online.

Fields of Study   The subject areas in which degrees and/or certificates are awarded.

Minimum Time on Campus   Any residency requirements the programs may have.

Admissions Requirements   The minimum requirements for admission to the programs, plus any policies in force for waiving them.

Cost   Either the total cost for completing the program or the per-credit tuition charge. These are basic costs that generally do not include books, travel if required, and fees normally charged by colleges for various services provided to students. Costs can be dramatically reduced if you have college credits that can be applied toward your program. Keep in mind that all institutions reserve the right to change their tuition and fees at any time, so consider this information as a general guide to what the program will cost you.

Transfer of Credits   Especially important to those who have already earned some college credits, this explains the policy concerning the maximum number of credits that can be applied to your degree or certificate. In all cases, transfer credits must be applicable to your program requirements, including electives.

Degree/Certificate Requirements   Outlines the minimum requirements that must be met to earn your degree or certificate.

Hardware/Software Requirements Describes any hardware or software specifications required to take online courses from each school.

Financial Aid Most but not all programs in the directory have been approved for federal and state student aid programs. In addition, some institutions have their own financial aid, usually in the form of scholarships, grants, and time payment plans.

Remarks Specific comments concerning the school or programs that are not covered by the previous captions.

FULL DESCRIPTIONS OF ONLINE DEGREE PROGRAMS

CALIFORNIA INSTITUTE OF INTEGRAL STUDIES

School for Transformative Learning
765 Ashbury Street
San Francisco, CA 94117
Contact Sarah Pinckney
(415) 674-5500, ext. 223
Fax: (413) 674-5555
E-mail: lcdsarah@aol.com

Accreditation Western Association of Schools and Colleges

Degree Offered Online Doctor of Integral Studies (Ph.D.)

Fields of Study Individualized studies program. Usually three years to complete course work plus time for dissertation. See Remarks for additional information.

Minimum Time on Campus All students are required to attend two week-long residencies, one at the beginning of the program, the other during the second summer; otherwise, all work is done online through the Electronic University Network and America Online.

Admissions Requirements A master's degree, although this can be waived for candidates with unusual promise who have demonstrated advanced learning in areas relevant to their program; a six- to ten-page autobiographical statement; two letters of recommendation; and a demonstrated capacity to learn and work both independently and collaboratively.

Cost Total cost, including travel and lodging, is approximately $30,000.

Transfer of Credits Not applicable.

Degree/Certificate Requirements Completion of 90 quarter hours of credit, attendance at the two residencies, and a doctoral dissertation.

Hardware/Software Requirements The only requirement is access to the Electronic University Network via America Online.

Financial Aid Standard federal and state programs.

Remarks Founded in 1968 as the California Institute of Asian Studies, CIIS residency and nonresidency programs focus on the scholarly and practical integration of philosophy, psychology, and spirituality. Approximately 800 students are currently enrolled in CIIS programs. All work for this degree, excluding the residencies, is done through online courses that comprise the core of the program. In addition, students may pursue independent study with faculty in other CIIS programs and with select mentors or adjuncts in their particular area of study. This program offers an innovative approach to studying and researching transformative change in individuals, groups, and cultures. Students have online access to library services, a learning community of other program participants, and a "student lounge" for informal and personal communications with CIIS students.

CALIFORNIA STATE UNIVERSITY, DOMINGUEZ HILLS

Humanities External Degree Program
1000 East Victoria Street
Carson, CA 90747

Contact On Line Assistant, Humanities External Degree Office
(310) 516-3743
Fax: (310) 516-3449
Web Site: http://dolphin.csudh.edu/~hux/huxindex.html
E-mail: huxonline@dhvx20.csudh.edu

Accreditation Western Association of Schools and Colleges

Degree Offered Online Master of Arts

Fields of Study Humanities. This is a broad interdisciplinary program that exposes participants to all areas of the humanities: history, literature, philosophy, music, and art.

Minimum Time on Campus None. This is a 100 percent external online degree program.

Admissions Requirements A bachelor's degree from a regionally accredited institution that need not be in the humanities and an undergraduate GPA of at least 3.0 for the last 60 semester credits or 90 quarter credits.

Cost Total cost is about $4,300, including books and related materials.

Transfer of Credits A maximum of 9 credits, which may include accredited correspondence courses.

Degree/Certificate Requirements Completion of 30 semester credits of work, including a final project.

Hardware/Software Requirements   A personal computer or hardwired terminal with a modem and monitor capable of displaying VT100 terminal emulation or ASCII; a communications package with Kermit protocol and text editor/word-processing software with the ability to save files as ASCII text; and a printer and storage method.

Financial Aid   Standard federal and state programs.

Remarks   This program is structured on a series of independent study courses developed by university faculty and an individually planned project that might be a thesis, an extended essay, or a creative endeavor such as a play, novel, musical composition, sculpture, or painting.

CITY UNIVERSITY

335 116th Avenue, SE
Bellevue, WA 98004

Contact   Boyd K. Smith, Director of On-Line Programs
(206) 637-1010, ext. 3829
(800) 426-5596, ext. 3829
Fax: (206) 277-2437
Web Site: http://www.cityu.edu/inroads/welcome.html
E-mail: bsmith@cityu.edu

Accreditation   Northwest Association of Colleges and Schools

Degrees Offered Online   Bachelor of Arts and Bachelor of Science

Fields of Study   Accounting, Art Appreciation/Art History, Business Administration, Computer Networking, Computer Programming, Computer Systems, Economics, Energy & Environmental Quality Management, Film History, Film Theory, General Studies, History, Humanities, International Studies, Journalism, Law Enforcement Administration, Literature, Management, Marketing, Mathematics, Philosophy, Political Science, Psychology, Sociology, Telecommunications Management

Minimum Time on Campus   None. These are 100 percent online external degree programs.

Admissions Requirements   High school diploma or equivalent and over eighteen years of age.

Cost   Tuition is $62 per credit for lower division courses and $176 per credit for upper division courses.

Transfer of Credits   A maximum of 135 quarter-hour credits may be transferred into these degree programs.

Degree/Certificate Requirements   Completion of 180 quarter-hour credits of work, of which 45 must be from City University, with a GPA of 2.0 or better.

Hardware/Software Requirements   An IBM-compatible (386 or later) or Macintosh computer with 4 megabytes of RAM and a 200-megabyte hard drive, a VGA monitor, and a 9600 baud modem are minimum requirements.

Financial Aid   In addition to standard federal and state programs, several university-sponsored scholarships are available.

Remarks   Founded more than two decades ago to serve working adults who want to build on their experience through education but cannot interrupt their careers to become full-time students, City University currently handles more than 30,000 enrollments annually. The university operates nearly two dozen instructional sites throughout the West Coast and Europe.

EAST CAROLINA UNIVERSITY

105 Flanagan
Greenville, NC 27858-4353
Contact   J. Barry DuVall, C.Mfg.E., Ph.D., Project Director
School of Industry and Technology
Department of Industrial Technology
(919) 328-4861 or (919) 328-6705
Fax: (919) 328-4250
Web Site: http://www.trp.sit.ecu.edu/
E-mail: itduvall@homer.sit.ecu.edu

Accreditation   Southern Association of Colleges and Schools
Degree Offered Online   Master of Science
Field of Study   Industrial Technology
Minimum Time on Campus   None. This is a 100 percent online external degree program.
Admissions Requirements   Undergraduate degree; at least three years of industrial/technical work experience; and the Miller Analogies or Graduate Record Examination.
Cost   Tuition is $3,240, exclusive of textbook and communications costs.
Transfer of Credits   All credits must be earned in the program.
Degree/Certificate Requirements   Completion of all twelve courses in the program.
Hardware/Software Requirements   A computer, modem, and local Internet provider.
Financial Aid   None currently available.
Remarks   The emphasis of this program is on industrial technology management and creative problem-solving in industry. It is divided into two

components, the common body of knowledge and a technical specialization in manufacturing.

EASTERN IOWA COMMUNITY COLLEGE DISTRICT

306 West River Drive
Davenport, IA 52801-1221
Contact   Margaret Baxter, Coordinator
(319) 359-7531
(800) 850-5443
Fax: (319) 359-8139
Web Site: http://ateec.kirkwood.cc.ia.us/
E-mail: mbaxter@eiccd.cc.ia.us

Accreditation   North Central Association of Colleges and Schools
Degree Offered Online   Certificate
Field of Study   Hazardous Materials Management
Minimum Time on Campus   None. This is a 100 percent external certificate program.
Admissions Requirements   Although open to all, the program is primarily intended for those already working in the hazardous materials field.
Cost   Tuition is $1,800 exclusive of textbooks and supplemental materials.
Transfer of Credits   All credits must be earned in the program.
Degree/Certificate Requirements   Completion of six courses for a total of 18 semester credits.
Hardware/Software Requirements   Any personal computer with communications ability and a communications software program.
Financial Aid   None available.
Remarks   The Hazardous Materials Technology Program originated with a grant from the U.S. Environmental Protection Agency. Its goal is to improve the job skills and level of knowledge of those working in the field or of students planning to enter the field of hazardous materials handling.

EMBRY-RIDDLE AERONAUTICAL UNIVERSITY

Department of Independent Studies
600 South Clyde Morris Boulevard
Daytona Beach, FL 32114-3900
Contact   Jim Gallogly, Manager, Graduate Programs
(904) 226-6263
(800) 866-6271

Fax: (904) 226-7627
Web Site: http://www.db.erau.edu/
E-mail: galloglj@cts.db.erau.edu

Accreditation   Southern Association of Colleges and Schools

Degree Offered Online   Master of Aeronautical Science

Fields of Study   Aviation/Aerospace Management or Operations specialization

Minimum Time on Campus   None. This is a 100 percent external degree program.

Admissions Requirements   Bachelor's degree from a regionally accredited college or university with an overall cumulative GPA of at least 2.5. Conditional admission may be granted to applicants with a GPA of 2.0 under certain circumstances.

Cost   Tuition is $10,260, exclusive of textbooks.

Transfer of Credits   A maximum of 12 graduate semester hours may be applied toward this degree provided they are from a regionally accredited college or university with at least a grade of "B" and are applicable toward an aeronautical degree.

Degree/Certificate Requirements   Satisfactory completion of 36 graduate semester hours of work, which is usually accomplished through twelve courses.

Hardware/Software Requirements   An IBM-compatible (386 or later) or a Macintosh, a modem with at least a 1200 baud rating, and a letter-quality printer capable of printing graphics; spreadsheet and word-processing software; a VCR and television for videotapes; access to CompuServe.

Financial Aid   Some financial aid is available.

Remarks   Embry-Riddle is highly regarded in the aviation/aerospace industry. The university offers a wide selection of other degree programs, both graduate and undergraduate, through its Department of Independent Studies. The primary format for these programs is correspondence-based courses.

INTERNATIONAL SCHOOL OF INFORMATION MANAGEMENT

501 South Cherry Street, Suite 350
Denver, CO 80222

Contact   Timothy Adams, Director of Admissions
(303) 333-4224
(800) 441-ISIM

Fax: (303) 336-1144
E-mail: admin@isim.com

Accreditation Distance Education and Training Council

Degrees Offered Online Master of Business Administration and Master of Science

Fields of Study Business and information management

Minimum Time on Campus None. These are 100 percent external degree programs.

Admissions Requirements A bachelor's degree from an accredited or state-approved institution, a resume demonstrating professional accomplishments and goals, an essay on reasons for attending ISIM, three letters of recommendation, and a passing score on the Graduate Management Admissions Test. Individuals without an undergraduate degree but having at least 20 years experience may be accepted.

Cost Approximate total cost for either degree program, including books and software, is $14,900.

Transfer of Credits A maximum of one-half the required 50 graduate credits can be transferred into either program.

Degree/Certificate Requirements Completion of 50 credits of work: 45 earned through online courses, and 5 earned by a final project.

Hardware/Software Requirements An IBM-compatible computer, 386 or higher, with Windows 3.1 or higher and a minimum of 4 megabytes of RAM, or a Macintosh Plus or higher computer; a 9600 or 14,400 baud modem; and an SVGA monitor. Software is supplied by the school.

Financial Aid The school offers payment plans, and will help students obtain funds from employer tuition reimbursement plans.

Remarks ISIM also offers courses in telecommunications and computer sciences. The school has won numerous awards for its distance learning courses, including the 1995 Best Distance Learning Program in Higher Education from the United States Distance Learning Association.

NEW YORK INSTITUTE OF TECHNOLOGY

P.O. Box 8000
Old Westbury, NY 11568-8000

Contact Beverly J. Tota, Director of Undergraduate Admissions
The On-Line Campus
(516) 686-7712
(800) 222-NYIT

Fax: (516) 484-8327
Web Site: http://www.nyit.edu/olc/

Accreditation   Middle States Association of Colleges and Schools

Degrees Offered Online   Bachelor of Arts, Bachelor of Professional Studies, and Bachelor of Science

Fields of Study   Behavioral Sciences, Business Administration, Interdisciplinary Studies

Minimum Time on Campus   None. These are 100 percent external degree programs.

Admissions Requirements   High school diploma or GED, unless you have already earned college-level credits at another institution. Applicants without a high school diploma should contact the On-Line Campus office for additional information.

Cost   Tuition is $295 per credit.

Transfer of Credits   A maximum of 90 credits may be transferred into these programs, including those earned through nontraditional methods such as portfolio assessment.

Degree/Certificate Requirements   Completion of 120 credit hours of work (Behavioral Sciences requires 128) with a GPA of at least 2.0. At least 30 credits must be earned at NYIT.

Hardware/Software Requirements   Any personal computer with a hard drive (for an IBM-compatible, a DOS or Windows environment is sufficient), a 14.4 modem, a word-processing program that creates files in ASCII, and a communications program such as Procom Plus or Microphone Mac.

Financial Aid   Standard federal and state programs apply.

Remarks   Based on computer conferencing among students and instructors, the NYIT On-Line Campus offers applicants a wide variety of ways in which to earn the necessary credits, including prior military or corporate training, proficiency examinations, and portfolio assessment.

ROCHESTER INSTITUTE OF TECHNOLOGY

Educational Technology Center
91 Lomb Memorial Drive
Rochester, NY 14623-5603

Contact   Susan M. Warner, Distance Learning Manager
(716) 475-7186
(800) CALL RIT
Fax: (716) 475-5007

Web Site: http://www.rit.edu/~smwetc
E-mail: smwet@rit.edu

Accreditation   Middle States Association of Colleges and Schools

Degrees Offered Online   Professional Certificate, Bachelor of Science, and Master of Science

Fields of Study   PC: Applied Computing and Communications, Data Communications, Emergency Management, Environmental Management, Health Systems Administration, Telecommunications Management, Voice Communications; BS: Applied Arts & Sciences, Electrical/Mechanical Technology; MS: Health Systems Administration, Information Technology, Software Development & Management

Minimum Time on Campus   None. These are 100 percent external degree programs.

Admissions Requirements   Professional certificate programs have no requirements, although it should be noted that they are designed for individuals already employed in the applicable fields. Undergraduate programs require an associate's degree or equal number of credits. Master's programs require a bachelor's degree with a minimum GPA of 3.0.

Cost   Tuition varies widely between the degree and certificate programs, so interested individuals must contact the institute directly.

Transfer of Credits   Each program allows a different number of transfer credits.

Degree/Certificate Requirements   Certificate programs require from 12 to 24 quarter-hour credits, undergraduate programs require 193 quarter-hour credits, and graduate programs require 48 quarter-hour credits.

Hardware/Software Requirements   Any personal computer with the capacity to emulate a VT 1000 with a modem and a VCR and television. Customized PacerLink software can be purchased from the RIT bookstore.

Financial Aid   Standard federal and state programs apply.

Remarks   Founded in 1829, RIT is the seventeenth largest private college/university in the nation. It has earned an international reputation for the quality of its educational programs.

ROGERS STATE COLLEGE

Claremore, OK

Contact   Electronic University Network
1977 Colestin Road
Hornbrook, CA 96044
(503) 482-5871
(800) 225-3276

Fax: (503) 482-7544
E-mail: eunlearn@aol.com

Accreditation   North Central Association of Colleges and Schools

Degrees Offered Online   Associate of Arts and Associate of Applied Science

Fields of Study   AA: Business Administration, Liberal Arts; AAS: Computer Programming, Computer Science

Minimum Time on Campus   None. These are 100 percent external degree programs.

Admissions Requirements   High school diploma or equivalent.

Cost   Tuition is $545 for each 3-credit course.

Transfer of Credits   It is possible to transfer up to 52 of the 64 required credits into these programs.

Degree/Certificate Requirements   Each program resulting in an associate's degree requires completion of 64 semester hours of work.

Hardware/Software Requirements   Any personal computer with communications capability and access to America Online.

Financial Aid   Standard federal and state programs apply.

Remarks   Rogers State College has been offering college-level courses online, via the Electronic University Network, since 1984.

RUTGERS, STATE UNIVERSITY OF NEW JERSEY

4 Huntington Street
New Brunswick, NJ 08903

Contact   Todd Hunt, Director of Distance Education
(908) 932-7914
Fax: (908) 932-6916
Web Site: http://scils.rutgers.edu/de/start.html
E-mail: thunt@scils.rutgers.edu/

Accreditation   Middle States Association of Colleges and Schools

Degree Offered Online   Certificate

Field of Study   Communications Management

Minimum Time on Campus   None. This is a 100 percent external online program.

Admissions Requirements   Open to all applicants.

Cost   Tuition is approximately $3,400.

Transfer of Credits   Not applicable.

Degree/Certificate Requirements   Successful completion of four courses in the program.

School of Communication, Information and Library Studies/SCILS	4 Huntington St. New Brunswick, New Jersey 08903

- <u>Degree Programs</u>
- <u>SCILS Administration</u>
- <u>School & Faculty Honors</u>
- <u>Research&Special Projects</u>
- <u>Services & Programs</u>
- <u>SCILS Computing Services</u>
- <u>SCILS Placement Services</u>

- <u>Faculty & Staff E-Mail</u>
- <u>Faculty & Students</u>
- <u>SCILS Catalog</u>
- <u>Sign our Guest Book</u>
- <u>Distance Education</u>
- <u>Professional Development</u>
- <u>Undergraduate Programs</u>

If you are using a Text Only browser click here: <u>SCILS</u>

You are visitor ░░░░░░ since April 19, 1996
This page last updated on July 4, 1996
Please direct any comments or questions to <u>*Jon Oliver*</u>

Hardware/Software Requirements Any personal computer with software capable of sending and receiving e-mail.

Financial Aid Not applicable.

Remarks Rutgers began offering its first online distance education course in 1995. Watch for more in the near future.

SALVE REGINA UNIVERSITY

100 Ochre Point Avenue
Newport, RI 02840-4192
Contact   Sister Leona Misto, Ed.D.
Director, Graduate Extension Study
(401) 847-6650
(800) 637-0002
Fax: (401) 849-0702
E-mail: mistol@salves.salve.edu   or   srugrieve@aol.com
Electronic University Network
(503) 482-5871
(800) 225-3276
Fax: (503) 482-7544
E-mail: eunlearn@aol.com

Accreditation   New England Association of Schools and Colleges
Degree Offered Online   Master of Arts
Field of Study   International Relations
Minimum Time on Campus   Attendance is required at a five-day residency on the campus. This may be done at any time during your course of study.
Admissions Requirements   An undergraduate degree from an accredited college or university. Applicants must also achieve a passing score on either the Graduate Record Examination, the Miller Analogies Test, or the General Management Aptitude Test.
Cost   Tuition is based on $300 per credit.
Transfer of Credits   A maximum of 6 credits of the required 36 can be transferred from an accredited institution.
Degree/Certificate Requirements   Successful candidates must earn 36 credits with a B+ average, attend one five-day residency, and take part in an exit interview.
Hardware/Software Requirements   Any personal computer with communications capability and access to America Online.
Financial Aid   Standard federal and state programs apply.
Remarks   The university was founded in 1934 by the Catholic Sisters of Mercy. It has been offering graduate extension programs since 1984.

THOMAS EDISON STATE COLLEGE

101 West State Street
Trenton, NJ 08608-1176

Contact   Sonja A. Eveslage, Ph.D., Director of Graduate Studies
(609) 292-5143
Fax: (609) 984-3898
Web Site: http://www.tesc.edu/
E-mail: mmarcus@call.tesc.edu

Accreditation   Middle States Association of Colleges and Schools

Degree Offered Online   Master of Science

Field of Study   Management

Minimum Time on Campus   All students are required to attend three residencies during the course of their program. At the start, there is a one-weekend orientation session. At midway and near completion, there are one-week residencies.

Admissions Requirements   A baccalaureate degree from a regionally ac-credited college or university plus demonstrated skills in self-directed and workplace learning.

Cost   The approximate total cost, including the residencies, is $16,813.

Transfer of Credits   A maximum of six credits may be transferred into this program, provided the student has successfully completed graduate-level course work in business or management at a regionally accredited college or university or earned those credits through the American Council on Edu-cation corporate courses.

Degree/Certificate Requirements   A total of 42 graduate credits, some of which are earned by attendance at the three residencies, and completion of a thesis.

Hardware/Software Requirements   A 486/33-MHz personal computer or a Macintosh with 8 MB of RAM and a 14.4 modem. Also needed is Internet access including a World Wide Web browser and an e-mail account.

Financial Aid   None available. It is expected that students enrolled in this program will be sponsored by their employers.

Remarks   Since 1972, more than 12,000 graduates have earned their asso-ciate and baccalaureate degrees from Thomas Edison. This is the nontradi-tional college's first graduate program. It was designed and tested with the support and partnership of major employers like AT&T®. The program was designed for experienced corporate managers who seek to advance their level of knowledge through a graduate program but prefer the distance learning approach.

THE UNION INSTITUTE

440 East McMillan Street
Cincinnati, OH 45206-1947

Contact The Graduate School
(513) 861-6400
(800) 486-3116
Fax: (513) 861-0779

Accreditation North Central Association of Colleges and Schools

Degree Offered Online Doctor of Philosophy

Fields of Study Interdisciplinary: individually tailored by each student

Minimum Time on Campus All students are required to attend a ten-day Entry Colloquium at the start of their program. These are held monthly at locations throughout the country and occasionally abroad. Students are also required to complete fifteen days at Graduate School–sponsored seminars, of which nearly forty are held each year, and ten days at peer meetings. This brings the total required residency to thirty-five days for the term of the program.

Admissions Requirements A master's degree, although occasionally an exception may be made for an individual who can clearly demonstrate achievements equivalent to that degree level; demonstrated ability to do self-directed work; and references from persons in your field of study.

Cost Tuition is $3,660 per semester. The average time in the program is three years and three months.

Transfer of Credits Because this program does not use credits as a means of measurement, it does not accept transfer credits, but recognition of prior learning can result in reducing the time it will take to earn a Ph.D.

Degree/Certificate Requirements A Learning Agreement that is designed by the student in collaboration with a doctoral committee specifies those learning activities that will be used. This agreement can make use of a wide variety of learning experiences, including courses at local universities, work done at libraries or museums, learning through professional associations and communication media, and numerous other nontraditional sources and methods. Graduation requires completion of all learning specified in the Learning Agreement, an internship, and a Project Demonstrating Excellence (PDE). The PDE can take many forms, depending on the student's field of learning. Examples are a publishable book, a unified series of essays or articles, a documented project of social change, or creative compositions.

Hardware/Software Requirements Communication maintained through the Union Network Bulletin Board. The requirements are any type of personal computer, any type of modem with a speed up to 19.2 kbps, and software that handles ANSI emulation. Connection is made through a toll-free telephone number.

Financial Aid Standard federal and state programs apply.

Remarks   This program is built around the concept of interdisciplinarity: that by working in more than one field, students have the opportunity to locate their ideas in a variety of frames of reference. The Union Institute was founded in 1964 by ten college presidents as the Union Graduate School. The name was changed when Union began offering undergraduate degrees. Of the 1,500 worldwide students enrolled in Union programs, 1,100 are in the Graduate School.

UNIVERSITY OF CALIFORNIA EXTENSION

2000 Center Street, 4th floor
Berkeley, CA 94704
Contact   Center for Media and Independent Learning
(510) 642-4124
Fax: (510) 643-9271
Web Site: http://www-cmil.unex.berkeley.edu
E-mail: cmil@violet.berkeley.edu

Accreditation   Western Association of Schools and Colleges
Degree Offered Online   Certificate
Field of Study   Hazardous Materials Management
Minimum Time on Campus   None. This is a 100 percent external program.
Admissions Requirements   Open to all.
Cost   Tuition is approximately $3,500.
Transfer of Credits   Not applicable.
Degree/Certificate Requirements   Successful completion of a series of nine courses.
Hardware/Software Requirements   Any personal computer with communications capability and access to America Online.
Financial Aid   Some partial scholarships are available.
Remarks   This is a nine-course program intended to provide participants with a thorough introduction to the foundations, principles, regulations, and technologies in the field of hazardous materials management.

UNIVERSITY OF MARYLAND UNIVERSITY COLLEGE

University Boulevard at Adelphi Road
College Park, MD 20742-1660

Contact Odin Wortman, Director, Open Learning Programs
(301) 985-7722
(800) 283-6832
Fax: (301) 985-4615
E-mail: open-learning@listserv.umuc.edu

Accreditation Middle States Association of Colleges and Schools

Degrees Offered Online Bachelor of Arts and Bachelor of Science

Fields of Study BA/BS: Behavioral Sciences, Computer Science, Computer Studies, Fire Science Management, Management, Management Studies, Paralegal Studies, Technology and Management

Minimum Time on Campus None. These are 100 percent external degree programs.

Admissions Requirements High school diploma or equivalent.

Cost Tuition for Maryland residents is $174 per semester hour; nonresidents are charged $195 per semester hour.

Transfer of Credits A maximum of 90 semester hour credits may be transferred into these programs.

Degree/Certificate Requirements Completion of 120 semester hours of work, of which at least 30 must be earned from the university, with a GPA of at least 2.0.

Hardware/Software Requirements Any personal computer, VGA or better graphics display, a modem, and access to the Internet. Tyco software is supplied by the university after enrollment.

Financial Aid Standard federal and state programs apply.

Remarks Using the software provided, you can access the university's online library services, online career planning, and online tutoring.

UNIVERSITY OF PHOENIX (ONLINE CAMPUS)

100 Spear Street, Suite 110
San Francisco, CA 94105

Contact Enrollment Department
(415) 546-9112
(800) 742-4742
Fax: (415) 541-7832

Accreditation North Central Association of Colleges and Schools

Degrees Offered Online Bachelor of Science, Master of Arts, Master of Science, and Master of Business Administration

Fields of Study BS: Business Administration, Business Information Systems, Business Management; MA: Organizational Management; MS: Computer Information Systems; MBA: International Business, Technology Management

Minimum Time on Campus　None. These are 100 percent external degree programs.

Admissions Requirements　Undergraduate programs require a high school diploma or equivalent and a minimum of 24 transferable credits from a regionally accredited institution. Graduate programs require a bachelor's degree from a regionally accredited institution and a GPA of at least 2.5 on the most recent 60 undergraduate credits and 3.0 on all prior graduate work. Applicants to all programs must be currently employed in or have access to an organizational environment appropriate to their studies.

Cost　Tuition is $335 per credit for undergraduate programs and $410 per credit for graduate programs.

Transfer of Credits　Undergraduate: requests to transfer credits from a regionally accredited institution are handled by an individual assessment. Graduate: a maximum of six credits may be accepted for transfer from a regionally accredited institution.

Degree/Certificate Requirements　Undergraduate students must complete 120 credits; graduate students must complete all courses in their program with minimum GPA of 3.0

Financial Aid　Standard federal and state programs.

Remarks　Communications between students and faculty and among students is conducted through private and study-group mailboxes.

APPENDIX A
Scholarships Online

There are over a dozen major companies that will assist college-bound individuals in locating scholarships and grants for which they might qualify. They charge fees that range up to $150 per search. While some provide their customers with extensive data that will help applicants apply for financial aid, others are little more than rip-offs selling only generalized information.

One of the most exciting innovations in the scholarship search field is a service called FastWEB. Run by a Chicago company named Student Services, Inc., which has been in business about nine years, this new service is offered online, and at no cost. Any Internet user can conduct a free scholarship search in Student Services' database of over 180,000 private scholarships. Student Services can be reached through their home page: *http://web.studentservices.com*.

Individuals in search of financial aid information will also find help at the following web sites. For information concerning financial aid programs sponsored by the United States Department of Education, turn to *http://www.ed.gov/prog_ info/SFA/Student Guide*. Global Network Navigator offers a free online book designed as an introduction to the subject of financial aid for students. The book can be found at *http://gnn.digital.com/gnn/wic/ed.24.html*.

APPENDIX B
A Virtual University in the Making

On June 24, 1996, the governors of ten western states announced plans to work together to establish a totally online university. Referring to their planned Western Governors' University as a "virtual university," they pledged to raise the money required to enable students to begin online courses toward earning online degrees sometime in late 1997.

Plans call for the new university to be integrated with the services of existing community colleges and state university systems in the ten states. This would make such vital facilities as college libraries available to online students of the new university.

The governors, each of whom has promised to contribute $100,000 to continue the planning process for Western Governors' University, foresee students turning in their papers via e-mail and taking part in online sessions. Although, as every reader of this book knows, there are numerous online courses and degree programs, this planned institution will be the first regionally accredited true "virtual university," having no campus, no classrooms, and no other facilities usually associated with a college or university. What the governors plan is to move one step further along the nontraditional educational path first taken by such institutions as Regents College and Thomas Edison State College.

The most current information on the progress of Western Governors' University can be found at *http://www.westgov.org/smart/vu/vu.html.*

Index

Abilene Christian University, 49
accounting, 74, 121, 155, 175, 194, 201–2
accreditation
    associations, 15, 16, 18–21, 92, 198
    defined, 15
    importance of, 10, 14–15, 73
    lack of, 17
    process, 15–16
    of professional specialized programs, 16,
      21
Accrediting Agency Evaluation Branch of the
    Office of Postsecondary Education, 15
adult learners, 4–5, 7–10
aeronautical science, 194, 204
Afro-American/African studies, 74, 141
Agnes Scott College, 49
agriculture, 74, 116–17
Albert Einstein College of Medicine, 49
Albertson College of Idaho, 50
Albion College, 50
Alderson-Broaddus College, 50
Alfred University, 50
Allentown College, 50
alternative education, 11–12
America Online, 49
American Association of Bible Colleges, 18

American Indian studies, 74, 142
American studies, 74, 142
Amherst College, 50
Andrews University, 50
Angelo State University, 50
animal sciences, 75, 106–7, 155
anthropology, 75, 143, 155–56, 172
Antioch College, 50
Appalachian State University, 50
applied arts and sciences, 194, 207
applied computing and communications, 194,
    207
architecture, 75, 175
Arizona State University, 50
art, 75, 94–95, 105, 143
art appreciation/art history, 194, 201–2
Association of Advanced Rabbinical &
    Talmudic Schools, 19
Association of Theological Schools in the U.S.
    & Canada, 19
Assumption College, 50
astronomy, 75, 122, 175–76
atmospheric science, 75, 176
Auburn University, 50
Augsburg College, 50
Augustana College, 50

Austin College, 50
Azusa Pacific University, 50

Baker University, 50
Ball State University, 50
Bard College, 50
Bates College, 51
Baylor College of Medicine, 51
Baylor University, 51
Beaver College, 51
behavioral sciences, 75, 136–37, 194, 206, 214
Belmont University, 51
Beloit College, 51
Berea College, 51
Bethany College, 51
Bethel College, 51
Bethel College and Seminary, 51
Bible colleges, 18
Binghamton University, 51
Biola University, 51
biological sciences, 75–76, 95, 122, 143, 156–57
Blackburn College, 51
Bloomsburg University, 51
Boise State University, 51
Boston College, 51
Boston University, 51
botany/plant science, 76, 122, 157
Bowdoin College, 51
Bowling Green State University, 51
Bradley University, 51
Brandeis University, 52
Bridgewater College, 52
Brigham Young University, 52
Brown University, 52
Bryn Mawr College, 52
Bucknell University, 52
Buena Vista University, 52
business college accreditation, 19
business, 76, 95–96, 108, 122–23, 137, 143,
    157, 194, 195, 201–2, 205, 206, 208,
    214–15
Butler University, 52

California College for Health Sciences, 52
California Institute of Integral Studies,
    199–200

California Institute of Technology, 52
California Institute of the Arts, 52
California Lutheran University, 52
California State Polytechnic University, 52
California State University, 52–53
California State University, Dominguez Hills,
    200–1
Calvin College, 53
Career College Association, 19
Carleton College, 53
Carnegie Mellon University, 53
Carroll College, 53
Case Western Reserve University, 53
Cedarville College, 53
Centenary College of Louisiana, 53
Central Connecticut State University, 53
Central Michigan University, 53
Central Missouri State University, 53
Central Washington University, 53
Centre College, 53
Cerritos College, 53
certificate programs, 193
Chapman University, 53
Charter Oak State College Credit Banking, 44
chemistry, 76–77, 97, 176
Chicago-Kent College of Law, 53
Christian Brothers University, 54
Christopher Newport University, 54
City University, 54, 201–2
City University of New York, 54
civil engineering, 77, 124
Clark University, 54
classical studies, 77, 157–58
Clemson University, 54
Cleveland State University, 54
Coe College, 54
Colgate University, 54
college degrees
    corporations and, 8, 23
    earning credits toward, 23, 43–44
    external programs, 3–10
    history of, 9–10
    importance of, 3, 4, 9
    nontraditional programs, 3–10
    online programs, 6, 9, 10, 194–215
    validity and recognition of, 13–18, 21–23

College of Aeronautics, 54
College of Charleston, 54
College of Eastern Utah, 54
College of New Rochelle's School of New
    Resources, 7
College of St. Benedict, 54
College of St. Scholastica, 54
College of the Holy Cross, 54
College of William and Mary, 54
Colorado College, 54
Colorado School of Mines, 54
Colorado State University, 54
Columbia College, 54
Columbia University, 55
communications, 77, 108, 116, 120–21, 133,
    137, 143–44, 158, 171, 176–77, 195,
    208–9
CompuServe, 49
computer science, 77–78, 108–9, 117, 124–26,
    138, 177, 195, 201–2, 208, 214–15. *See
    also* applied computing and
    communications
Concordia College, 55
Connecticut College, 55
Cornell University, 55
Cornerstone College, 55
corporate training and degree programs, 8,
    23
correspondence courses, 5–6, 11, 13, 23
Council on Recognition of Postsecondary
    Accreditation (CORPA), 15, 17, 21, 73
course locator, 74–92
credits
    banking, 43–44
    earning, 23
    transferring, 198
Creighton University, 55
criminology/criminal justice, 80, 158
cultural studies, 80, 109, 138, 144

Dakota State University, 55
Dana College, 55
Dartmouth College, 55
data communications, 195, 207
degree plans, 34–35
degree programs, 194–215

Denison University, 55
DePaul University, 57
Diablo Valley College, 57
diploma mills, 14, 15
Distance Education and Training Council, 19
distance learning courses, 11
Dixie College, 57
Dordt College, 57
Drake University, 57
Drew University, 57
Drexel University, 58
Duke University, 58
Duquesne University, 58

Earlham College, 58
East Carolina University, 58, 202–3
East Central University, 58
East Stroudsburg State University, 58
East Tennessee State University, 58
East Texas State University, 58
Eastern Illinois University, 58, 93
Eastern Iowa Community College District,
    203
Eastern Michigan University, 58
Eastern New Mexico University, 58
Eastern Oregon State College, 58, 93–104
Eastern Washington University, 58
economics, 80–81, 97, 117, 126, 158–59,
    177–78, 195, 201–2
Edinboro University of Pennsylvania, 58
education courses, 81, 93, 97–98, 144–45, 159,
    178
electrical/mechanical technology, 195, 207
electronic mail, 6, 24
Embry-Riddle Aeronautical University, 58,
    203–4
emergency management, 195, 207
Emmanuel College, 58
Emory University, 58
Emporia State University, 58
energy and environmental quality
    management, 195, 201–2
English, 81, 98, 145
entomology, 81, 145, 159
environmental studies, 81–82, 118, 126–28,
    145, 178–79, 195, 207

exam preparation, 30–31
experiential learning, 5, 12, 23
extension and adult education courses, 82, 160
external programs
    accreditation, 10
    adult learners and, 9
    advantages of, 3, 9
    defined, 10, 11
    faculty advisors, 8
    history of, 5
    recognition of, 21–23
    residency requirements, 12
    success in, 24–25
    traditional programs and, 10

faculty directed courses, 11
Fairfield University, 58
Fast WEB, 217
Fayetteville State University, 59
Federation of Regional Accrediting
    Commissions of Higher Education, 15
Ferris State University, 59
film, 82, 109–10, 118, 128, 195, 201–2
finance, 82, 160
financial aid, 199, 217
fire science management, 196, 214
Fisk University, 59
Florida A&M University, 59
Florida Atlantic University, 59
Florida Institute of Technology, 59
Florida International University, 59
Florida State University, 59
foods and nutrition, 82, 107
Fort Hays State University, 59
Franklin and Marshall College, 59
Fullerton College, 59
Furman University, 59

Gallaudet University, 59
Gannon University, 59
gender studies, 82, 110
general studies, 196, 201–2
geography, 82, 98, 160–61, 179
geology, 82, 128, 161, 179
George Mason University, 59

George Washington University, 59
Georgia Institute of Technology, 59
Georgia Southern University, 59
Georgia State University, 59
gerontology, 83, 179–80
Gettysburg College, 60
GMI Engineering & Management Institute, 60
goal setting, 39–41
Gonzaga University, 60
Goshen College, 60
Goucher College, 60
Governors State University, 60, 104–5
Graceland College, 60
graduate programs, 22–23. *See also* college
    degrees
Grand Valley State University, 60
grants, 217
Grinnell College, 60
Gustavus Adolphus College, 60

Hahnemann University, 60
Hamilton College, 60
Hamline University, 60
Hampden-Sydney College, 60
Hampshire College, 60
Hampton University, 60
Hanover College, 60
Harding University, 60
Hartwick College, 60
Harvard University, 61
Harvey Mudd College, 61
Haverford College, 61
hazardous materials, 196, 203, 213
health systems administration, 196, 207
Heidelberg College, 61
Hendrix College, 61
Hillsdale College, 61
Hiram College, 61
history, 83–84, 110, 135–36, 145–48, 162,
    172–73, 180, 196, 201–2
Hobart and William Smith Colleges, 61
Hofstra University, 61
home pages, 47, 49
home study institutions, 19
Hope College, 61

How to Earn a College Degree without Going to College (Duffy), 6
How to Earn an Advanced Degree without Going to Graduate School (Duffy), 6
Howard University, 61
humanities, 196, 200–2
Humboldt State University, 61
Huntington College, 61
hypertext transfer protocol (http), 49

Idaho State University, 61
Illinois Institute of Technology, 61
Illinois State University, 61
Incarnate Word College, 61
independent study programs, 11, 13. *See also* external programs; nontraditional programs
Indiana Institute of Technology, 61
Indiana State University, 61
Indiana University, 61
Indiana University of Pennsylvania, 62
Indiana University Purdue University, 62
industrial technology, 196, 202–3
information management and technology, 196, 207
innovative programs. *See* nontraditional programs
integral studies, 196, 199–200
interdisciplinary degree programs, 196, 206, 212–13
international business, 196, 214–15
International School of Information Management, 62, 204–5
international studies, 196, 201–2, 210
Internet, 47–49
Internet for Dummies, The (Levine and Baroudi), 48
Internet for Kids (Pedersen and Moss), 48
Iowa State University, 62
Ithaca College, 62

Jacksonville State University, 62
Jacksonville University, 62
James Madison University, 62
Johnson C. Smith University, 62

Jones College, 62
journalism, 84, 148, 163, 196, 201–2

Kalamazoo College, 62
Kansas State University, 62, 105–7
Keene State College, 62
Kent State University, 62
Kenyon College, 62
Kutztown University of Pennsylvania, 62

La Sierra University, 62
LaFayette College, 62
LaGrange College, 62
Lake Forest College, 62
Lake Superior State University, 63
Lamar University, 63
language, 84, 148–49, 180–82
Lasalle University, 63
law enforcement administration, 196, 201–2
Lawrence University, 63
learning contracts, 34–37
Lehigh University, 63
Lewis & Clark College, 63
liberal arts, 197, 208
Liberty University, 63
Linfield College, 63
linguistics, 84, 111, 182
literature, 84–85, 111–12, 128, 136, 163–64, 173–74, 182–84, 197, 201–2
Lock Haven University, 63
Louisiana College, 63
Louisiana State University at Baton Rouge, 63
Louisiana Tech University, 63
Loyola College, 63
Loyola Marymount University, 63
Loyola University, 63
Lycoming College, 63

Macalester College, 63
management, 85–86, 118, 128–29, 138–40, 149, 164, 197, 201–2, 211, 214
Mankato State University, 63
Marist College, 63
marketing, 86, 118–19, 129, 140–41, 164–65, 197, 201–2

Marlboro College, 63
Marquette University, 64
Marshall University, 64
Mary Washington College, 64
Maryland Institute, 64
Massachusetts Institute of Technology, 64
Massachusetts Maritime Academy, 64
mathematics, 86, 98–99, 129, 133–35, 141, 184–85, 197, 201–2
McNeese State University, 64
Medical College of Georgia, 64
Medical College of Ohio, 64
Medical College of Wisconsin, 64
Medical University of South Carolina, 64
Mercer University, 64
Mercyhurst College, 64
Meredith College, 64
Messiah College, 64
Metropolitan State College of Denver, 64
Metropolitan State University, 64
Miami University of Ohio, 64
Michigan State University, 64
Michigan Technological University, 64
Middle States Association of Colleges and Schools, 15, 20
Middle Tennessee State University, 65
Middlebury College, 65
Midwestern State University, 65
Millersville University, 65
Millsaps College, 65
Milwaukee School of Engineering, 65
Mississippi College, 65
Mississippi State University, 65
Missouri Western State College, 65
Monmouth College, 65
Montana State University, 65
Montclair State University, 65
Monterey Institute of International Studies, 65
Moravian College, 65
Mount Holyoke College, 65
Mount Union College, 65
music, 86, 112, 149–50, 185
Muskingum College, 65

National Commission on Accrediting, 15
National Technological University, 65

National University, 65
New England Association of Schools & Colleges, 20
New England Culinary Institute, 66
New Jersey Institute of Technology, 66
New Mexico Institute of Mining and Technology, 66
New Mexico State University, 66
New School for Social Research, 66, 107–15
New York Board of Regents, 14
New York Institute of Technology, 66, 205–6
New York University, 66
Nicholls State University, 66
noncollegiate education, 6
nonresidential programs, 11, 13
nontraditional programs
  accreditation, 10
  adult learners and, 7–8, 9
  advantages of, 3, 42
  deciding about, 24–25, 39–43
  defined, 11, 13
  goal setting, 39–41
  history of, 4–5
  recognition and value of, 8, 21–23
  study skills, 28–31
  success in, 24–25
  time considerations, 31–34, 40, 41–42
  traditional programs and, 10
  types of, 5–6, 23
North Carolina Agricultural and Technical University, 66
North Central Association of Colleges & Schools, 20
North Central Bible College, 66
North Dakota State University, 66
North Dakota University System, 66
Northeast Louisiana University, 66
Northeast Missouri State University, 66
Northeastern State University, 66
Northern Arizona University, 66
Northern Illinois University, 66
Northern Michigan University, 66
Northwest Association of Schools & Colleges, 20
Northwest Nazarene College, 66
Northwestern College, 66

Northwestern Michigan College, 67
Northwestern State University, 67
Northwestern University, 67
Nova Southeastern University, 67
nursing, 87, 150
nutrition, 87, 99, 129–30, 186

Oakland University, 67
Oberlin College, 67
Occidental College, 67
oceanography, 87, 186
office administration, 87, 99–102
Ohio Northern University, 67
Ohio University, 67
online programs
    adult learners and, 9
    computer conferencing and, 6, 24
    electronic mail and, 6, 24
    formats, 6, 24
    as independent study, 13
    success in, 10
    teacher-student relationship in, 40
    and "virtual university", 218
Ontario Institute for Studies in Education, 67
organizational management, 197, 214–15

Pacific Lutheran University, 67
paralegal studies, 197, 214
philosophy, 87, 102, 112, 119, 130, 150, 165,
    186–87, 197, 201–2
physical education/health, 88, 102, 130,
    165–66, 187
political science, 88, 102–3, 112, 130, 150–51,
    166–67, 187–88, 197, 201–2
PQRST reading method, 28
prerequisites, 92
proficiency examinations, 5, 23
psychology, 89–90, 103–4, 112, 119, 130–31,
    151–52, 167–69, 188–90, 197, 201–2

rabbinical and Talmudic schools, 19
Raritan Valley Community College, 67, 116
reading, 27, 28–30
Regents College, 5
Regents Credit Bank, 44
religion, 90, 119, 131–32, 152, 190

Rochester Institute of Technology, 67, 206–7
Rogers State College, 207–8
Russian, 90
Rutgers, State University of New Jersey,
    208–9

Salveregina University, 210
San Jose State University Continuing
    Education, 67
scholarships, 217
School of Education—Nagoya University, 67
School of Graduate Studies and Continuing
    Education, 67
science, 90, 112–13
Seattle Pacific University, 67
social work, 90, 152, 169–70
sociology, 90–91, 113–14, 120, 132, 136, 153,
    170, 190, 197, 201–2
software development and management, 197,
    207
Southern Association of Colleges & Schools,
    20
Southern Illinois University at Carbondale,
    116–17
Southern Maine Technical College, 67
special education, 91, 171
statistics, 91, 153, 190–91
study skills, 27–34
Survey Q3R reading method, 28

technology and management, 197, 214–15
telecommunications management, 197, 201–2,
    207
theater arts, 91, 114
theological schools, 19
Thomas Edison State College, 67, 117–20,
    210–11
Thomas Edison State College Credit Banking,
    44
time considerations, 31–34, 40, 41–42
trade and technical schools, 19
tuition, 92

unaccredited colleges and universities, 17, 18
Union Institute, The, 211–13
United States Department of Agriculture—
    Graduate School, 67, 120–21

United States Department of Education, 15, 17, 21, 73, 217
University of California, 70
University of California Extension, 70, 121–32, 213
University of Georgia, 70
University of Idaho, 70
University of Illinois at Urbana, 70, 132–35
University of Iowa College of Education, 70, 135–36
University of Kansas, 70
University of Maryland University College, 136–41, 213–14
University of Michigan, 70
University of Minnesota, 70, 141–54
University of Missouri, 70, 154–71
University of Nebraska, 70
University of North Dakota, 70
University of Northern Colorado, 171
University of Oklahoma, 70
University of Phoenix, 214–15
University of Santa Cruz's Online Catalog, 70

University of Tennessee Continuing Education, 70
University of Texas, 70, 172–74
University of the State of New York, 13–14
University of Utah, 70
University of Virginia, 70
University of Washington, 71, 174–92
University of Winnipeg, 71
University of Wisconsin, 71

"virtual university", 218
voice communications, 197, 207

Web browser software, 49
Web site directory, 47–71
Western Association of Schools and Colleges, 21
Western Governors' University, 218
World Wide Web, 48–49
writing, 91–92, 104, 114–115, 132, 153–54, 174, 191–92